KEY ELEMENTS
OF THE ZODIAC

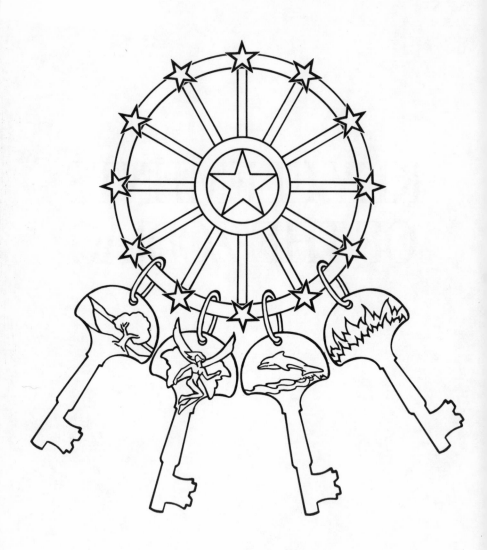

KEY ELEMENTS OF THE ZODIAC

BY

VIRGINIA KAY MILLER

Stellar Communications
PO Box 1403
Nashua, New Hampshire 03061

ACKNOWLEDGMENTS

I would like to express deep thanks to my dear friend, Catherine Morley, whose unswerving commitment to me on both a personal level and a professional level is greatly appreciated. As a true best friend, Catherine has always been there to give me spiritual and moral support for my astrological work. In particular, I want to thank her for her dedicated efforts as Chief Editor which included *many* hours editing and proofreading this manuscript.

A special thank you for editing also belongs to my wonderful brother-in-law, Louis Federici, who generously offered to edit my manuscript despite his extremely busy schedule. He was an excellent editor with an exacting eye for detail and an optimistic, enthusiastic attitude. It was a pleasure to work with him.

I would also like to acknowledge my first astrology teacher, Amy Klainer. She believed in me and knew I would become an astrologer, even when it seemed an impossible dream to me. Starting me on my astrological journey, she introduced me to a spiritual and psychic approach to astrology.

The next five individuals I would like to acknowledge were all instrumental in the production of *Key Elements Of The Zodiac*.

First, I would like to thank my terrific student, Sheri Fairbend, for the design concept of the astrological key chain and for her genuine appreciation for my astrology teachings.

Second, I would like to thank Mark Winzeler, President of Winzeler Typography, and Gail Clarke for the cover design. I also want to thank Mark for his friendship, support, and willingness to advise me in all aspects of production.

Third, I want to credit photographer Dace Winzeler for the picture on the back cover and her help during the photo session.

Fourth, I want to express a great deal of thanks to the crew at Amanuensis who formatted the book's text using desktop publishing technology. In particular, I want to credit President Diane Romagnoli who designed the book's innovative and bold look.

Last but not least, I want to acknowledge the printer, Puritan Press, and President Fred Lyford whose advice has been instrumental to the success of this project.

DEDICATION

This book is first dedicated to my Aquarian parents, Sally and Bob Miller who helped my dream come true. Their lifelong commitment as loving parents and caring friends will always be appreciated.

It is also dedicated to my friend and my second astrology teacher, Richard A. Greene, who introduced me to the Elemental Invocations which are contained in this book. I want to thank him for sharing with me his pioneering research into astrology and human consciousness. His advanced teachings have made a great deal of difference in my personal spiritual growth and have contributed to my astrological expertise.

TABLE OF CONTENTS

FOREWORD

Much of the information that an accurate, professional astrologer develops is through the knowledge and use of the basics. One such basic is the use of the elements - fire, water, air and earth. These elements are evident in the astrological chart and when coupled with insight and awareness, provide incredible skills and insight to the astrologer.

The purpose of Virginia Kay Miller's book, *Key Elements Of The Zodiac*, is to offer a strong background in the elements of astrology (Part One) and in the elements of the zodiac (Parts Two–Four). Virginia has long recognized the need for the astrological student to understand the basics completely and only then move to advanced techniques of astrological delineation.

Key Elements Of The Zodiac is a necessary book and should be required reading for all astrological students, teachers and professionals. This book has a wealth of information and techniques that can give the astrologer valuable insights on both the basic and advanced levels of astrological delineation.

As an educator, Virginia enjoys teaching her first love — Astrology. This will become evident as you read the book. You will learn more about Astrology from many different perspectives such as Mythology and the different types of Astrology, i.e., political astrology. In addition, you will learn about the elements of fire, water, air and earth in a way that I have seen no other astrologer teach in my twenty-two years as a professional astrologer. Finally, you will get a greater insight about the signs from Ms. Miller's original theory and research — that each sign has a secondary modifying element. Again, this is valuable information that I have not seen or heard of from any other astrologer.

All in all, you are in for a great treat. Enjoy this book and may your life never be the same!

Richard A. Greene
Author of *The Handbook of Astral Power*
Nashua, New Hampshire
April 6, 1988

★ ▬▬▬▬▬▬▬ INTRODUCTION

The Importance Of Learning The Basics

O nce I met a woman who had been studying astrology for seven years. Even though she had been studying for a long time, she felt blocked and frustrated when she tried to interpret an astrology chart. Thinking that her problem was a lack of advanced astrological information she asked me to teach her a course on planetary aspects. I refused, but offered to start her in my beginning class which would give her an in-depth foundational awareness of the zodiac. She protested and asked why, after seven years of study, she should take a beginning course. Very bluntly, I told her that if she was having that much trouble figuring out planetary aspects after seven years of study, then she was missing some very important and basic information.

In the end, she took the course and later admitted that I had been right. Not only had she missed some of the basics of astrology, but in all her years of study she had only acquired a mental perspective of astrology. She had all these astrological facts in her mind but she couldn't *feel* their energies or intuitively sense their possibilities. By the end of my course she was beginning to finally feel the astrological energies and this deepened and grounded her astrological information. New insights started to come forward as a whole new awareness of the zodiac began to emerge.

To those readers who are impatient astrology students anxious to learn about the planets, the houses, and chart interpretation, I offer these words of advice — before you jump into the more advanced levels of astrology, it is essential that you have a strong and deep understanding of the zodiac. The zodiac is the backbone of astrology and therefore, without a foundational understanding of the zodiac, your astrological knowledge will be limited and will eventually reach an insurmountable impasse.

The purpose of this book and the ones that will follow is to help you become acquainted with the zodiac on a feeling, intuitive level as well as on a logical, intellectual level. In this book, we will start at the very beginning by exploring how to approach your astrological studies. Then we will move on to study the elements — the building blocks of the zodiac. All too often I feel that the elements have been ignored as astrology students rush off to study planetary aspects and house interpretations. Consequently, like the lady mentioned at the beginning of the Introduction, too many students lose their way in their astrological studies, simply because they don't have a solid, foundational understanding of the basics of the zodiac.

By the time you finish this book, you will not only have a strong awareness of the elements, but perhaps an understanding of the zodiac that could surpass students who have studied for years but who have superficially rushed through their astrological studies.

Have fun as you read *Key Elements Of The Zodiac*, and always give yourself the opportunity to play with the elemental exercises before you turn to the Appendix. Not only will you learn more this way, but you will be practicing what all good astrologers do naturally — thinking for yourself.

In the end, no book can teach you astrology. A book can only put you on the path. You are the one that walks the path. I hope you enjoy your journey.

Best Wishes,

Virginia Kay Miller

★■■■■■■PART ONE

ELEMENTAL CONCEPTS YOU SHOULD KNOW

■■■■■■■■■■■ **CHAPTER ONE**
An Introduction To Key Concepts

■■■■■■■■■■■ **CHAPTER TWO**
The Myths About Astrology

■■■■■■■■■■■ **CHAPTER THREE**
How To Learn Astrology

★ ▬▬▬▬▬▬▬▬▬▬▬▬▬▬ **CHAPTER ONE**

An Introduction To Key Concepts

Before you begin to read this book, answer the questions below just to gauge where you are at this moment in your astrological awareness.

1. What is astrology?

2. Why do you want to study astrology?

Okay, now that you've given some extra thought to the study of astrology and why you are choosing to explore it, let's begin.

Astrology is more than a superficial, cocktail party ice-breaker; it is a language that offers a rich, symbolic understanding of the workings of individual and collective human consciousness. If you succeed in becoming astrologically fluent, then astrology offers you an inner doorway into a new level of consciousness that will enrich your life through unlimited psychological and spiritual insights.

Why an individual studies astrology will vary from person to person. It is important to recognize the purpose behind your studies because this will not only determine how far you go with astrology but will also determine what areas of astrology you study.

Everyone knows that astrology can be used to understand individual personalities, but did you know it can also be used to understand sociological, political and economic trends? And for the more metaphysically concerned, astrology offers a wholistic, philosophical and spiritual system that can unlock a greater awareness of life. In the next few pages, let's take a look at a few of the different types of astrological frameworks you can explore.

ASTROLOGY AND PSYCHOLOGY

The astrological signs are widely recognized by the public as personality archetypes. Yet, how many people today are really aware of how much astrology and psychology are connected? Probably not many at all, even though increasing numbers of contemporary astrologers have not only taken psychology courses in college (I did), some even have undergraduate and graduate degrees in psychology! It's not surprising to find out that psychologists sometimes hire astrologers when it is a fact that Carl Jung, one of the founding fathers of psychology, studied and used astrology.

So what exactly is the relationship between modern day astrology and psychology? Certainly both **sciences** seek to understand and explain human behavior. However, when a psychologist classifies various personalities and predicts probable behavior, it is accepted as scientific fact. Unfortunately, when an astrologer speaks of those same archetypes and refers to them in terms of zodiacal or planetary archetypes, this is often dismissed as occult or treated as simply fun entertainment.

Despite its occult labelings today, astrology has been accepted as a basic, integral part of life for most of recorded history. In contrast, psychology is a new discipline of study which was not accepted until after World War II.

Until astrology is given the recognition it deserves, I feel psychologists will be credited with breakthroughs that are already known facts to astrologers. For example, remember when Gail Sheehy's book *Passages* was first published. She became famous because of her *new* theory that there are seven year cycles of growth. I remember my reaction well, "So, what's new? Astrologers have always known about the seven year cycles of change."

I look forward to the day when people in the media and the public at large, give astrologers as much respect as they give psychologists. Putting the validity of daily horoscopes aside for the moment, let me just say that I'm glad my local newspaper places the horoscopes on the advice page instead of the comics page. It may be a small step, but it's still one step closer to that day when astrology is presented and recognized, like psychology, as a credible and useful study of human behaviour.

───────── ASTROLOGY AND SOCIOLOGY

One of the ways that I enjoy studying astrology is by watching how sociological trends tie in with current astrological planetary cycles.

For example, why did the women's movement take off in the early 1970's? To an astrologer the answer is obvious. In the fall of 1971 the planet Pluto entered the sign Libra. Pluto is a planet that affects our mass consciousness and whenever it moves into a new sign it sets off whole new sociological trends. Astrologers associate Pluto with a transformational death and rebirth energy (remember Pluto was the Roman god of death!). Quite simply it is a planet of power and its power affects the individual and the collective consciousness. Libra is ruled by Venus, a planet associated with women. Put transformational Pluto with the Venusian ruled sign Libra and it's no wonder that women, on a mass level, started to mobilize to gain power (Pluto) for women (Libra).

It's also interesting to note that Libra is the sign associated with marriage and the 1970's were a time where marriage was challenged, not only by the increasing divorce rate but also by new concepts such as open marriages, group marriages and gay marriages.

Getting back to the women's movement, remember how in the early 80's Betty Friedan and other feminist leaders talked about how the movement was entering a new stage? Was it really a coincidence then that the Pluto in Libra cycle was ending? (Pluto entered Scorpio at the end of 1983.) I think not.

Or to take another example, let's look at what happened when Neptune was in Sagittarius from January 1970 to January 1984. Neptune is a planet associated with mysticism and spirituality; Sagittarius is a sign associated with philosophy, religion and long distance travel. Remember how many people were involved in spiritual pursuits during that time period? Many people thought you had to go to India to find true spiritual awareness (Sagittarius's travel influence). However, whether you followed an Eastern guru, joined Scientology, or became a reborn Christian (to mention just a few possibilities), you were acting appropriately under the influence of the Neptune in Sagittarius transit.

By January 1984 when Neptune transited into the sign Capricorn, people started following a new dream — the materialistic, yuppie dream. Neptune is the planet associated with illusion and fantasy; Capricorn is the sign associated with corporate success and status. Think how many people have idealized and even worshipped money, status and success in recent years. Through the media we have been saturated with get-rich-quick schemes and dreams of yuppyville heaven. A couple of years ago I read an article that said only 4% of the population were yuppies — but you'd never know that judging by how many people are chasing the yuppie pot of gold (albeit through credit cards).

With Saturn (the planet of realism and practicality) entering Capricorn in February 1988, I think you'll start to see that the fantasy money bubble we've all been living in will burst. Saturn will make us confront the reality of our Neptunian fantasies. (Because the influence of new major transits is often felt months before the actual transits occur, I think this contributed to why people panicked during

October 1987. On some level of awareness, people are becoming more aware that the feel good economic period is ending.)

Finally, before I leave this section, let's take one more look at the Pluto in Scorpio transit which started at the end of 1983 and will continue through 1995. Pluto is the planet associated with death and with sex. It rules Scorpio, the sign associated with death and sex. Is it really any coincidence then, that we now have the fatal disease, AIDS, which is transmitted sexually? Again, I think not. When transits end, issues are resolved. Therefore, I think that by the end of this transit in 1995, a vaccine or some sort of cure will have been developed.

ASTROLOGY AND POLITICS

United States

Just as an individual has a birth chart that expresses the nature of the individual personality, so too does a country have a birth chart that expresses the nature of its mass consciousness.

For example, the United States was born as a country on Independence Day, July 4, 1776. Due to the very strong position of Uranus (the planet of inventions and technology) in America's chart, we have always been a highly inventive and scientific country.

However, despite our strong mental nature, with four planets located in the sign Cancer, we are a very emotional country and we respond to attacks on America with emotional outbursts instead of intellectual reasoning. Add to our emotional nature the negative Cancerian trait of clannishness and you have a country that retreats into itself (like a crab into its shell) and refuses to see the realities of other people who live outside our English-speaking, Judeo-Christian framework.

On a more positive level, the Cancerian mothering urge moves us to help those in the world less fortunate. But the flip side of the coin is that we try to save the world instead of realizing that no one country, not even the United States, can save the planet by itself.

Political Currents and Presidential Campaigns

Astrology can also be used to understand the political currents of a nation, and if presidential candidates were smart they would listen to astrologers to find out the astrological mood of the country.

In 1980, Saturn, the planet associated with old age, was extremely strong in America's chart. And who did we elect? The oldest president in American history — a grandfatherly Ronald Reagan.

In 1984 the transits of Jupiter and Neptune were creating an illusory feel good psychological mindset in the American public. People didn't want to hear the truth, especially if it painted a bleak picture of the future. Walter Mondale might have been right about the problems of the deficit but people weren't in the mood to listen to him. Too bad Mondale didn't have astrologers on his campaign; he could have been forewarned!

Even the emergence of the character issue in the 1988 presidential campaign was predictable, given the conjunction of Uranus and Saturn in the sign Sagittarius. With Uranus (the planet of upsets) and Saturn (the planet of responsibility) placed in Sagittarius (the sign of ethics and morality), this spelled trouble for any candidate who was not absolutely squeaky clean.

When Uranus and Saturn moved into the sign Capricorn in mid-February 1988, the character issue seemed to lose importance (no coincidence!). However, Saturn and Uranus will both go back into Sagittarius for the last half of the year and when it does, the character issue will reemerge as one of the presidential election's biggest issues.

Before I leave the Uranus-Saturn conjunction in Sagittarius, let me also point out that Sagittarius is the zodiac sign associated with religion. Consequently, it's not surprising that two presidential candidates are ministers. It was because of this transit that I publicly predicted in December 1987 that Pat Robertson and/or Jesse Jackson should not be underestimated.

1988 Presidential Candidates

You can tell a lot about a presidential candidate's character and even their issue priorities just from knowing their personal astrological chart. Without going into great detail, let me just give you a few sun sign examples. George Bush is a Gemini and Geminis are famous for "beating around the bush." The seemingly unflappable Michael Dukakis is a Scorpio, a sign known for its ability to hide their inner feelings. When Jesse Jackson talks about equality and social justice, he is expressing his Libran nature; Libra is a sign known for its fairness and concern with justice.

Before I end this section on the 1988 presidential race, I'd like to point out that an astrological chart can be made for any political event, including the announcement of a presidential campaign. Astute politicians should consider the planetary positions of their campaign announcement date because it will set in motion their campaign's direction and general tone.

Gary Hart should have consulted an astrologer before he announced in the spring of 1987. His campaign chart indicated there were secrets in his personal life. Considering the rumors that existed from his previous campaign, this was not a propitious chart and he should have chosen a different announcement date.

On the Republican side, George Bush's announcement chart shows that whether or not he is hiding anything about the Iran-Contra affair, he will be perceived as keeping secrets. Perhaps he should have chosen a different announcement date as well.

Astrologers in Political History

While the idea of politicians using astrologers may strike some of you as funny or weird, actually it is quite the historical norm. Astrologers have always been in the thick of politics throughout Western civilization. Queen Elizabeth I, Hitler, and Catherine de Medici are only a few rulers who engaged the services of astrologers. I hope that someday historians will take note of this and give the astrological (and psychic) political counselors their rightful place in history. After all, if astrologers have always advised politicians throughout the course of history, then it's possible that our past heritage is due in large part to astrologers!

—————————ASTROLOGY AND ECONOMICS

A person with a strong background in economics and in astrology could make a fortune. For just as sociological and political trends can be perceived before they happen, so too can business cycles be anticipated before they occur.

As we saw in earlier pages, the yuppie phenomenon blossomed around the time when Neptune transited into the sign Capricorn in January 1984. An astrologically-minded entrepreneur with extra cash would have spotted the yuppie phenomenon and been ready to captialize on it just as it began.

Using astrology to understand the economic cycles is nothing new. In ancient Babylonia, astrologers looked to the skies for information on a country's future prosperity. Today, people in the astrological know can use astrology to improve their financial status.

Yes, you can even use astrology to buy and sell stock! In fact, one of my first jobs after I graduated from college was working for a brokerage firm. One of the firm's partners told me that his father, who had also been a partner, had successfully bought and sold stocks according to astrology!

I don't have a background in economics; I'm not an expert in this branch of astrology. However, armed just with my knowledge of astrology and the United States's natal chart, I have been publicly disagreeing for years with all the economic experts who have been saying that America's economy was healthy and doing just fine. I know that America's fantasy world will come to a rude awakening in 1988 and 1989 when the planets Uranus and Saturn enter the sign Capricorn and aspect America's natal planets located in the house of money.

In basic terms, the rollercoaster economic movements we saw in the fall of 1987 are only a preview of the bust/boom cycles that will follow. It's too bad that economists don't study astrology — then they wouldn't be caught by surprise!

ASTROLOGY AND HEALTH

When doctors take the Hippocratic oath, how many of them know that Hippocrates was a firm believer in astrology? In fact, Hippocrates believed that a healer should know his patients' astrological makeup since certain herbs were good for certain signs and bad for other signs.

Most medical practitioners today probably don't even give astrology a thought. However, back in the mid-70's a student in one of my astrology classes told me a very interesting story. She was a nurse who worked at a very prestigious Boston hospital and according to her, the unofficial policy at her hospital was to postpone, when possible, operations until after a full moon. Apparently doctors had realized that operations done during full moons had more complications.

I'm not a medical astrologer since I have no background in health and medicine. However, an old astrology tradition states that the signs are connected to different parts of the body. By knowing a person's sun sign, you can be aware of where an illness could *potentially* manifest. For example, the breasts are associated with the sign Cancer and it is interesting to note that Nancy Reagan is a Cancer and had breast surgery.

Of course, medical astrology is a lot more complicated than just knowing someone's sun sign. (Just because you are a Cancer does not mean that you will need breast surgery!) Keeping this in mind, try a beginning exercise by reading through the following partial list of astrological/body correlations and see if it makes sense for you and your friends and family.

Astrological/Body Correlations

Aries - Head	*Libra* - Kidneys
Taurus - Throat	*Scorpio* - Sexual Organs
Gemini - Lungs	*Sagittarius* - Thighs
Cancer - Stomach, Breasts	*Capricorn* - Knees
Leo - Heart, Spine	*Aquarius* - Ankles
Virgo - Intestines	*Pisces* - Feet

_____ THE ZODIAC AS PHILOSOPHICAL KEYS

And finally, the zodiac can be studied as a complete philosophical system that holds the keys towards understanding the process of human development on individual and collective levels.

To those readers who are new to astrology, the ordering of the signs may seem arbitrary and meaningless. But make no mistake, the signs' specific ordering is but one of many clues which unlock the wisdom they contain. As there is a logic behind every philosophy, so too there is a logic behind the structure of the zodiac.

For example, why does Libra, the sign pertaining to marriage, come after Virgo, the sign of self perfection? The answer is that you cannot have a positive, meaningful love relationship with another individual until you have become complete within yourself.

Let's look at another example. Why does Sagittarius, a sign associated with religion, follow Scorpio, the sign associated with death? What comes to my mind right away is how many people do not turn to religion until there is a death or a threat of death in their circle of loved ones. Death (Scorpio) often leads to concerns with the spiritual world (Sagittarius).

The wisdom of astrology is like an ever flowing fountain of knowledge. No matter where you are in your stage of development, you can drink from the fountain and in the process, tap into your higher mind through the philosophy of astrology.

★ ━━━━━━━━━━ CHAPTER TWO

The Myths About Astrology

TRUE OR FALSE?

1. Astrology takes away your free will.
2. Astrologers are uneducated fortunetellers.
3. Daily horoscopes are accurate representations of astrology.
4. Two people born under the same sign will be exactly alike.
5. Astrologers only give general personality profiles.
6. All astrologers will give you the same information.
7. Only superstitious people go to astrologers.
8. Astronomy is superior to astrology.

If you answered true to any of these questions, then you are laboring under some inaccurate information. If you answered true to every question, then be prepared to restructure your whole perception of astrology.

Congratulations to those of you who accurately answered false to every question. I'm glad you understand some basics about the use and practice of astrology.

1. False: *Astrology Takes Away Your Free Will.*

Once when I was on a radio talk show, a caller asked me about the question of free will. I responded by asking him if he felt he was limited by the fact that he had inherited his body from his parents' genes. After all, because of his parents' genes, he had inherited a certain type of body, hair color and eye color, etc. What type of body he inherited from his parents was beyond his control but, as I pointed out to him, how he took care of his body was up to him and how he chose to use his free will.

Just as our parents' genes give us our physical inheritance, so too does our astrological birth chart give us our psychological inheritance. What we do with our personality's strengths and weaknesses is up to our free will.

Perhaps a few astrologers are around who still believe in an absolute astrological destiny. I don't think most contemporary astrologers believe in fatalistic astrology. I feel *very* strongly about this point because of what happened to me the first time I had an astrological reading.

It was in the spring of 1971 and the astrologer was well known. However, in my short thirty-minute reading, she disregarded my free will. At the time I was nineteen, attending Smith College (a private women's college), and still waiting for some sort of social life to appear. When she told me that I would marry in two years but the marriage would end in divorce, I thought, "Why even bother dating?"

To her credit, it is true that I was involved in a serious relationship when I was twenty-one. However, through my intuition I had known almost from the beginning of the relationship that I would not marry this person. Intuitively I knew it wouldn't work and so I didn't marry him.

This astrologer went wrong in a couple of ways. First, she didn't talk to me about free will and about my choices in life; she just laid out an irrevocable destiny of a broken marriage. Second, she failed to recognize and take into account my strong, intuitive nature, which is pretty evident from my astrological chart.

On a positive level, however, this woman gave me two lessons which I've never forgotten:

1) **Astrology does not take away free will.**
2) **Astrologers should not disregard the free will of their clients.**

Astrology does not create your personal power. You create your own personal power and bring it to your astrological blueprint. Remember something that I tell all my clients — **you always have the choice to use your power, misuse your power, or ignore it altogether.**

2. False: *Astrologers Are Fortunetellers.*

A long time ago a new astrology client came to my apartment for a consultation and was openly astonished how middle class and burgeois my home looked. Apparently he had expected a candlelit apartment with mysterious vibrations! (Who knows what I was supposed to look like.) He obviously didn't know that a professional astrologer is a counselor who probably has a college degree and maybe even a graduate degree in psychology.

Let's face it — a double standard exists. When astrologers predict events we are lumped into the category of fortunetellers. However, when a weatherman predicts a storm, a sportscaster predicts the winner of the World Series, or a political analyst predicts the outcome of a presidential campaign, then their predictions are considered reliable and newsworthy.

Why is there a double standard? Just as the weather, sports, and political experts are respected and paid for their predictions, so too should astrologers be respected and paid for their predictions.

Perhaps one reason the double standard exists is because people who mistakenly think astrology negates free will are threatened by astrology. Denying the validity of something that scares you is a common psychological game we all play with ourselves.

Or perhaps astrologers have been placed in the fortunetelling category because to the lay person, it is uncanny how astrologers can accurately predict the timing of an individual's life cycles. At best we are called mystical prophets; at worst we are called gypsy fortunetellers. I certainly don't think either label is appropriate, since like psychologists, astrologers are students of the science of human consciousness.

Astrology is the science of planetary energies and their impact on human behaviour. Astrologers are scientists — just as much as psychologists and metereologists are scientists. And just like a meteorologist who predicts a storm based on current weather conditions at the moment, so too does an astrologer predict a life event based on current astrological conditions.

To insist that astrologers are fortunetellers while psychologists, political analysts, and meteorologists are professional experts is hypocritical. The public should either refer to all predictive experts as fortunetellers or treat astrologers with the same respect that other predictive experts receive.

3. False: *Daily Horoscopes Are Accurate Representations of Astrology.*

Of course it's ridiculous to say that all Aries on a given day will lose money or that all Sagittarians on that same day will fall in love. Life isn't that simple and neither is astrology. Contrary to a horoscope's seemingly simplistic approach, astrologers believe that every person is a complex, individualized entity with his own destiny to fulfill.

Unfortunately, many people mistakenly judge the validity of astrology by what their local newspaper's horoscope says. And when two different horoscope columns say different things, naturally the skeptic cries out, "See, I told you that astrology is worthless!"

However, daily horoscopes do not by any means represent the full potential of astrology. What the public should realize is that daily horoscopes are nothing more than the commercialization of astrology. Horoscope columns are *extremely* limited in scope, but unfortunately, that's what the newspapers print. If you'd like to see a more in-depth column, then by all means write your paper's editor and express your views.

On a positive level, at least horoscopes have brought an awareness of astrology to the public at large. But from a negative level, daily horoscopes have misrepresented astrology by making it seem as if astrology is nothing more than vague, generalized two-line personality descriptions. Nothing could be further from the truth.

Seriously, if you want astrological advice, don't go to the comic section of the newspaper, go to a professional astrologer who can give you individualized attention and information.

4. False: *Two People Born Under The Same Sun Sign Will Be Exactly Alike.*

Although the sun signs are widely recognized as personality archetypes, it is important to understand that astrology does not begin and end with the sun signs.

Yes, people who have the same sun sign will share certain traits and motivations, but as I mentioned in the previous section, people are complex, individualized entities. Astrologers acknowledge the full spectrum of the human personality by analyzing a client's complete astrological makeup. According to astrological thought, the sun sign expresses the basic integrated self, while the moon and the planets express specific personality characteristics. Astrologers study not only the sun's astrological position (commonly called the sun sign), but also the zodiacal placements of earth's moon and the eight other planets in this solar system. (Some astrologers even analyze the influence of particular asteroids and stars.)

When you consider how the moon and the planets are always in motion, it's easy to understand how two people who share the same sun sign, but who were born in different years, will have different planetary aspects. Consequently, even though two people have the same sun sign orientation, they will have different personality traits because of differences in the positioning of the moon and the planets.

Even being born on the same day doesn't insure that two people will be exactly alike. To give you an example from my personal life, I have a "twin cousin" named Susan. I call her my "twin cousin" because we were born on the same day, in the same year, and in the same city! (No mean feat — sometimes I think she and I were born "twin cousins" just so I'd have another astrology story to tell!)

I remember that when we were growing up Susan and I would sometimes talk about our similarities. Even though we were different in our self expression, there was a core level that was connected. As we grew into our adult years, we lived in separate states and rarely saw each other. But in the fall of 1986, after years of not being in touch, we had the opportunity to reconnect at a family wedding. Right away our Scorpio nature came out and we were involved in a deep, intense conversation. I laughed when Susan said, "I'm so glad you're here! You're the only other person in the world who is as intense as I am!"

However, like twins, we weren't born at the same exact time; I was born in the morning and she was born at night. Due to the big difference in our birth times, there are a number of differences in our astrological makeups. First, we don't share the same moon sign because the moon changed signs between our births. So while I have a Moon in Leo, she has a Moon in Virgo. I may think of being vegetarian at times, but Susan, with her health conscious Moon in Virgo, is a vegetarian.

Second, because of our different birth times, the setup of our astrological charts are completely different. I have Sagittarius rising; she has Cancer rising. Most of my planets are located in the upper half of my chart, while most of her planets are located in the lower half of her chart. Consequently, I am more extroverted and career-minded and she is more introverted and family oriented.

Let me emphasize one last point. Even if you could locate two individuals with the *exact* same astrological chart, they would not be destined to be exact carbon copies of each other.

Why not? **Astrology does not create consciousness, it only reflects the consciousness that you create. You are the creator and at every moment you are creating your consciousness through the choices you are making with your free will.**

5. False: *Astrologers Only Give General Personality Profiles.*

Due to the many misconceptions about astrology and the emphasis on sun signs, it's not surprising that some people believe astrology only provides very general personality profiles. And to the seemingly logical skeptic, it's just too much of a leap of faith to believe that one's birth data provides detailed personality information.

Even clients of mine who are at least already open enough to astrology to have a reading, are still amazed at the detailed accuracy of their readings. On a number of occasions I've had clients who have expressed their wonderment after a reading because I know them even better than their best friend! And yet, all they gave me to work with was their birth data! I remember one client who was trembling because she was so amazed by the precise details of her reading. She just couldn't fathom how I could know her so well!

An astrologer can give you very specific information, not only about your personality, but also about your current and future life issues. Don't make the mistake, however, of thinking that this means that an astrologer will know exactly how many children you have, how long you've been at your job or what your favorite hobby is.

Remember, an astrology chart is like a roadmap, but you – not the planets — drive yourself through life. When you go to an astrologer, he won't know exactly how you've been using your free will, although he *will* know specifically what issues you are working on — now and in the future.

6. False: *All Astrologers Will Give You The Same Information.*

Once a new client told me that she had been going to different astrologers for twenty years and she had been devastated by the negative readings she had always received. Although I understood where these other astrologers were getting their information from my client's chart, I also felt that their interpretations showed a limited understanding of astrology and a lack of counseling ability. Instead of helping the client understand how she could change her negative patterns, they just predicted negative future happenings.

In my consulation with her we went over her personality patterns from a negative and a positive level. I counseled her on the importance of taking responsibility for creating her life and gave her an awareness of how she could begin to choose a better life. After the reading she told me that my approach to astrology was completely different than what she had experienced with other astrologers.

Does the difference in the quality of the astrological readings mean that astrology doesn't work? Absolutely not! It does mean, however, that an astrologer is only as good as his level of consciousness. And just as the medical field has a mix of good and bad doctors, so too does the astrological field have astrologers with different degrees of competency.

How an astrologer perceives astrology and how he communicates his perceptions to a client depends totally upon his personal awareness and his personal power. For example, if an astrologer has a doom and gloom consciousness, then he tends to see his clients' charts through his doom and gloom mindset. On the other hand, if an astrologer is a positive and spiritually-oriented individual, then he will most likely see the potential in the clients' charts and motivate them to realize their highest potential.

Another thing to keep in mind is just as there are many different types of doctors, so too are there different types of astrologers. Depending on what your needs are, you might go to different astrologers. For instance, if you want advice on how to invest your money, you would go to an astrologer who has a strong working knowledge of economics and business. If you'd like an astrologer to tell you about your past lives, then go to an astrologer who is able to psychically tune into your past lives by focusing in on your astrology chart. (Although some astrologers believe there is a link between astrology and reincarnation, not all astrologers believe in this connection.)

I believe that whatever happens to you is a reflection of your consciousness and so you will always find the right astrologer for you at that moment in your life. And in reverse, an astrologer's clients are a reflection of that astrologer's consciousness. For example, many of my clients are educated, already open to consciousness, and looking to improve their lives (as I am). In fact, many times if I have a certain issue to work through in my life, I'll have a number of clients who are working through the same issue. Whether or not they realize it, my clients are my teachers as well.

7. False: *Only Superstitious People Go To Astrologers.*

If you think only uneducated, misguided, superstitious people go to astrologers — guess again. People from all walks of life and all types of professions have astrological consultations.

Just for fun, I decided to make a quick list of some of my clients' occupations. Here's what came to my mind: television executive, florist, writer, lawyer, teacher, real estate agent, radio and television celebrity, corporate manager, musician, psychotherapist, and a former professional hockey player.

As you can see from this short list, my clients are educated, intelligent, active individuals. Most of them sincerely want to improve their lives and many of them are open, to varying degrees, to New Age ideas.

Why do people go to astrologers? Most of my clients are in some sort of crisis or life transition when they come to me. Sometimes they have already talked to their family, friends, and therapist. They're still confused since friends and family are biased and not always able to offer objective advice. By coming to me, an astrologer who only knows their birth information, they can get an honest and objective appraisal of their life situations.

Other times people come to me because they want to see if their astrology chart will back up their personal intuitions and feelings. These people are already self-directed, but it's comforting for them to find out that astrology verifies what they know already to be true. Many times, the astrology consultation serves to strengthen their determination and resolve to change their life.

Occasionally I get clients who are just curious. For the most part, though, the people who come to me are seeking answers and are willing to take responsibility for their lives. For my clients, an astrological reading is a way of focusing in on their life blueprint so that they can more effectively use their free will and actualize their potential.

8.   False: *Astronomy Is Superior To Astrology.*

How many people living today realize that astrology was once a commonly accepted and established fact of life? This has changed now and while modern thought accepts astronomy as a legitimate field of study, it dismisses astrology as nonsense. Astronomers reject the concept of astrology as an outrageous idea. "How could the planet Saturn influence events on earth?" they ask. And yet, in the same breath, they support studies which show that sunspot activity affects earth's climate. And the sun is 93 million miles away! In a similar fashion, scientists accept as fact that the moon has a large influence on earth's ocean tides. And yet, even though a large percentage of the human body consists of water, the idea that the moon could affect human behaviour seems preposterous!

Hopefully, at some point in the future, astrology and astronomy will be recognized as sister sciences. Their differences are not as great as one might think. Basically, it boils down to a different perspective on reality. Concerned with the physical aspect of life, astronomers investigate the solar system's outer material composition. In contrast, astrologers are concerned with the nonphysical layers of consciousness that create the physical reality. They investigate the solar system's inner psychic forces.

Astrology is not astronomy's foolish young sister. If anything, she is astronomy's wise and older sister. Astrology studies the primal forces of consciousness; astronomy studies the material end result. Astrologers can intuitively discover new information; astronomers can only discover what our technology is capable of sensing and measuring.

Let me suggest these final thoughts.   Perhaps modern astronomy's recent advances are a measure of our growing global awareness of the interrelationship and unity of all living things. Perhaps astronomical discoveries are dependent upon the level of our global consciousness. Could it be that a planet cannot be physically discovered until it has first been psychically discovered? Perhaps the astronomer William Herschel was not acting as an individual but as an agent of the global consciousness when he discovered Uranus in 1781. Thought provoking, isn't it?

★ ▬▬▬▬▬▬▬▬▬▬▬▬▬ CHAPTER THREE

How To Learn Astrology

Many people think that the only way to learn astrology is by reading lots of astrology books. However, years later, after reading countless books on astrology, they still feel like a beginner without a firm grasp on the subject. And no wonder! All they know is what others have written and if the information differs from one book to the next, they are at a loss to figure out which author is right. The following story illustrates this point.

Once I met an individual who claimed he was an astrologer. I soon realized this wasn't true. How did I know? During our conversation he asked me what I thought of a particular aspect in his birth chart. He proceeded to quote what various authors had written and now he wanted my opinion. I asked him what he thought it meant and he just shrugged his shoulders. I knew then that he wasn't an astrologer because he had no astrological insights of his own. Consequently, he had no real understanding of astrology, let alone of his own chart! He should have called himself an astrology student, not an astrologer!

This is not to say that astrology books are useless. Certainly, I would not be writing this book if I thought so. However, most of my astrological information did not come from astrology textbooks. At the time I entered this field (1971) there were very few informative astrology books in print and I had to turn to other sources. In the process, I learned much more than I would have if I had just limited myself to the material in astrology books. I have personally used all of the following astrological learning strategies to expand my own astrological awareness. Try whatever feels right for you.

___ HOW TO APPROACH LEARNING ASTROLOGY

As a language which expresses the universal archetypes of the collective unconscious, astrology is not a subject which can be thoroughly understood through the use of the logical, rational mind. Although it is possible to intellectually understand astrology by examining the logical progression in meaning of the signs and planets, this is quite different from KNOWING their essences. Intellectual thinking and experiential, intuitive knowingness are two very different ways of perceiving. Intellectual thinking creates pros and cons and either/or situations. The individual I mentioned at the beginning of this chapter was stuck in an intellectual rut and that's why he couldn't make sense out of the different authors and their conflicting views.

In contrast, knowingness brings in a very real sense of certainty; there is no question regarding the validity of the information. While thinking gives birth to ideas, knowingness gives birth to realizations. And there's a great deal of difference between the two!

No matter what method you use to research astrology, always use your intuition. Also, always trust whatever you sense is right, even if it does not completely agree with current astrological methods. Today, as a new level of consciousness is descending upon earth, the field of astrology is in the throes of change. New ideas and new theories are constantly redefining astrological systems.

___ OBSERVATION AND COMPARISON

One of the best ways to learn astrology is to observe it in action in everyday life. I've studied astrology for seventeen years and I still learn new information by connecting my life, other peoples' lives, and even political, sociological and economic events back to astrology. Because I have always challenged myself to understand the astrological connections of life events, my mind is trained to automatically perceive and think through an astrological mindset.

Even if you are a beginning student, you can start to train your mind to perceive the astrology in your life and to learn (and use) new astrological information. Don't worry that you're just a beginner – start with the information you know.

For example, most people know that life can get a little crazy during the week building up to a full moon. You can start by noticing how you are feeling during a full moon week. Talk to your co-workers, family and friends to see how their lives are being affected by the full moon. Notice how people are driving. I usually notice that people tend to make careless or downright dangerous driving maneuvers during the week of a full moon! In short, keep your eyes open and you'll learn a lot from everyday experiences.

Another good place to start is by finding out the pertinent astrological data for your family, friends and co-workers. Take note of their moods, their communication patterns and their relationships with others. Then ask yourself how it fits with their astrological makeup.

If you don't know what sign a person is, challenge yourself to figure it out. I remember one instance where I observed a fellow co-worker and figured out that he was a Virgo. It really wasn't that hard — the clues were pretty obvious. This man had worked at the same company for 50 years. He arrived at work at 8 am (one hour early), ate lunch at 4 pm, left at 6 pm (2 hours later than closing time), and brought work home! He was a hard worker and yet despite all his dedication, he wasn't a partner or a top level manager! What else could he be but a sacrifical, workaholic Virgo? True to his Virgoan skeptical nature, he was extremely surprised when I told him I knew his sign!

When you try to figure out a person's sun sign, treat it as a fun, learning game and don't judge yourself in terms of success or failure. Above all, don't worry about being wrong. Remember, you might just be tuning into the person's rising sign or their other planetary aspects.

And one last note of caution — don't let yourself be trapped by skeptics who want you to prove astrology by guessing their sign. First of all, being able to pick out someone's sun sign doesn't prove astrology. Second, even if you are successful, the skeptic will still find another reason to disbelieve astrology. Third, I've yet to meet a skeptic who knows his own chart. So if you came up with his rising sign instead of his sun sign, then you will just get invalidated by the skeptic, instead of feeling encouraged by your ability to sense a certain zodiacal emphasis in his personality.

Last of all, remember that the purpose of observing astrology in everyday life is to stimulate and challenge your astrological awareness. No matter how you go about doing it, the more you use astrology and incorporate it into your everyday worldview, the more your understanding of astrology will grow and expand.

ASTROLOGY CLASSES

Of course, a good way to study astrology is by taking classes from a professional astrologer. If you don't know of any teachers in your area go to your local health food store or metaphysical book store — many times they have bulletin boards where astrologers can advertise their services. Or look in the yellow pages (that's where I advertise), or in the classified sections of newspapers, especially alternative-oriented newspapers. If you listen to your intuition and trust your unconscious you will be led to the right teacher at the right time.

The way that I became involved in astrology was totally a working of my Higher Self. Some might say that I accidentally fell into astrology, but I'd disagree.

Prior to the summer of 1971 I had already been going through a lot of soul searching. I was in college and was trying to figure out who I was, what life was all about and what I should be doing with my life. My psychic abilities were starting to turn on and I had a very strong psychic impression that I should not spend the summer of 1971 at my parents' home. I didn't know exactly why; I just knew that I had some very important changes to go through and I had to be free to discover what they were, without my parents' influence.

Listening to my strong psychic feeling, I took a volunteer social work job in Boston and consequently had a chance to explore the different opportunities that the Boston/Cambridge area offered. I decided to take a pottery course but when I went to register, the course was filled. When I saw that an astrology course was still open, I signed up for it.

At the time I had no conscious idea how significant that course would be to me. But from the very first class I was totally enthralled. By the end of the course when my teacher, Amy Klainer, told me I would become a professional astrologer, I was excited beyond words and also scared, too, that I couldn't do it!

Looking back on it, no wonder I had such a strong psychic impression to spend the summer away from my parents' home. I had no conscious knowledge that I wanted to be an astrologer and yet, it was time for me to meet my destiny and I found an astrology teacher whose approach to astrology was exactly what I needed to get me on my astrological path. So, if you know you'd like to study astrology, you're one step ahead of where I was when I started my studies. Let your inner awareness guide you, just as I let my inner awareness guide me, and you'll find the right teacher.

One important point to remember, though — **no matter how terrific the teacher is or how much he or she imparts, in the end it is only your personal interpretation and understanding of astrology that counts.** If all you do is memorize a list of facts, then that's all you'll have — a list of facts. **But if you use your personal power to bring meaning to astrology, then you will enter the realm of astrological wisdom and you'll be able to understand and use the transformational power of astrology.**

CONVERSATIONS

A second way to expand your astrological awareness is through conversation with other astrology-minded individuals. Many times astrology students (especially beginning students) reach a point where, no matter what they do, they just can't seem to go beyond their own astrological perspective. Conversations with others may help you go beyond the plateau. Another person may offer you a brand new piece of information or he may simply rephrase a familiar idea in a slightly different fashion which then opens up a whole new level of understanding. I remember one summer where I engaged in numerous astrology raps with a good Gemini friend. She and I went on and on for hours. I inspired her and she inspired me and the ideas were flying! I think I learned as much, if not more, from our conversations than I had learned in the four previous years.

Talking out astrology ideas or asking questions is also important for another reason. Many times people have learned a lot of information, but the information is stuck inside their mind. Since they are not communicating it, they may underestimate the amount of knowledge they do have. They may feel that even after years of study, they don't really know anything! However, once they begin to talk and to share their information they realize that they actually do know quite a bit about astrology. This realization gives the self confidence and inspiration to keep on learning more.

Also, it seems as if communication is a process of housecleaning. The more you communicate old knowledge, the more room there is for new ideas and concepts. For example, many times when I am in the process of reading a chart or teaching a class, whole new intuitive insights will come to my mind as I communicate (or houseclean) my familiar information.

BEGIN WITH YOUR CHART

The best place for beginning astrology students to start is their own natal chart. By comparing your personality and life experiences with the information in your chart, you will begin to realize their connections and at that point you will begin to **KNOW** astrology. For example, a person with Mercury in Virgo does not have to strain to remember the appropriate keywords of this planetary placement. He knows from his own personal experience that he is a detailed, mental perfectionist with an overactive, analytical mind.

Before I leave this section, let me just point out that life is really a process of self discovery. As you grow and change your own self awareness, your understanding of your natal chart and astrology as a whole, will expand and deepen. That's why, even though I've been studying astrology for seventeen years, I'm still learning.

MYTHOLOGICAL STUDIES

Another good way to expand your astrological knowledge is to study the ancient Greek and Roman mythologies. Let's say you want to learn more about the sign Scorpio and its ruling planet Pluto. Read up on the Roman myths concerning Pluto (who was also called Hades in the Greek myths). Pay attention to his character, his powers and his relationship with the goddess Proserpine (known as Persephone in the Greek myths). Ask yourself how all these different particulars fit in with the character of the sign Scorpio and the planet Pluto. Maybe a new insight will emerge. Or maybe an old insight will be deepened.

To take an example, legend has it that Hades owned a helmet which rendered him invisible when he wore it. Now, how does this piece of information relate to the energies of the sign Scorpio and the planet Pluto? Scorpios, as well as individuals with a strong Plutonian influence in their chart, are often very secretive and hidden people. They are in a sense invisible, because like Pluto, the god of the underworld, they are very private and do not usually show their true feelings and thoughts.

Or, to take a second example, read the legend about the Greek god Hermes (Mercury), who as a young child succeeded in cleverly stealing Apollo's sacred cattle. Mercury is the planet that rules Gemini so you might ask what does this mean about Geminis? Certainly not all Geminis are thieves, but they are known for their clever mind.

──────────────PHILOSOPHICAL STUDIES

For those readers who have a strong, foundational understanding of the zodiacal and planetary archetypes, I suggest the study of philosophy to enlarge your astrological scope. Philosophy, like astrology, examines reality through the focus of various archetypal perspectives. Also, as I mentioned earlier, astrology can be approached as a complete philosophical system. Each sign has its own viewpoint or philosophy on life. And just as no one philosophy holds the key to truth, so too, no one sign is better than another sign. Each sign, like each branch of philosophical thought, merely expresses a part of the world.

When you are reading philosophy, ask yourself "What are the basic premises behind this philosophical system?" Then, once you have established this, try to figure out which sign corresponds with that philosophical perspective. In this way, you can learn a lot about the nature of that sign and those born under its influence. However, don't feel as if you have to limit your analysis to one sign. Sometimes a particular philosophy may express the ideas of a number of signs. Other times it may only touch on one specific level of a sign.

── PSYCHOLOGICAL & SOCIOLOGICAL STUDIES

In addition to reading philosophy, you can also research astrology by studying psychology and sociology. To illustrate this, let me show you some of the sources I used years ago to research the sign Sagittarius.

Since Sagittarius is the sign associated with positive thinking and religion, I read *The Power of Positive Thinking* by the Christian writer Noman Vincent Peale. I further investigated the religious aspect of Sagittarius by reading *Religion And The Unconscious* by Ann and Barry Ulanov, *The Sociology of Religion* by Max Weber and *Sociology and The Study of Religion* by Thomas F. O'Dea. Since Sagittarius is also the sign concerned with mythology (religious and secular), I also decided to research the nature of myths, their purpose and influence. To this end, I read *Man And His Symbols* by the famous late psychologist Carl G. Jung, *Ancient Myths and Modern Man* by Joseph L. Henderson and *Myth and Reality* by Mircea Eliade.

Certainly this is not a complete reading syllabus for the Sagittarius sign. There are many other books you could read as well. My personal understanding of Sagittarius is an accumulation of years of study — I was a religion major in college and studied sociology, philosophy and psychology as well. However, don't worry if you don't have such a background. Although I initially drew on a lot of books that I read in college, my reading research for Sagittarius went beyond my college curriculum. If you have no idea what books to read, I suggest you do the following.

Let's say you want to research the sign Sagittarius. As we have already seen, there are a number of topics that fall under this sign. Pick one subject or keep a number of possibilities in your mind. Then go to a good bookstore or library and browse through the appropriate categories. If one book really strikes you, pick it up and look at it. Listen to your inner feelings and your intuition — they will guide you to the right books. Even if you are not sure how a particular book will help you, if you feel that there is something in the book that is relevant to your search, then read it! Don't expect every book to bring you numerous revelations. Some books have done that for me. Others have only offered a small piece of the puzzle.

———————— TAROT AND QABALAH STUDIES

Another excellent way to increase your astrological awareness is through the study of two other metaphysical systems: the Tarot and the Qabalah. Each card in the Tarot deck has an astrological correspondence. For those of you who are more artistically inclined, meditation on the Tarot cards might be an effective way to obtain new astrological insights.

The Qabalah is an ancient spiritual doctrine. At the foundation of the Qabalah are ten spheres, each of which is associated with a planet. Connecting the ten spheres are twenty-two paths and each path is connected to a particular Tarot card. Even numerology is intertwined with astrology in the Qabalah!

————————————MAGICKAL* INVOCATIONS

My work with the elements and my love for them was really ignited by my magickal work that I learned from Richard Greene in the mid-70's. He taught me how to travel into the elemental planes and contact the elemental beings. The exercises you will learn in Chapters 4-7 are simplified versions of invocations that he teaches.

Once you know how to invoke the elements you can feel their energies firsthand and talk to the elemental beings to gather information on astrology. For example, in researching Cancer, I've used elemental magick to invoke the mermaids (the water elementals) and then asked them questions about Cancer. As the beings of the water element, they can also tell you about Scorpio and Pisces, the other two water signs.

Likewise, in preparing material on the earth sign Virgo I've invoked the gnomes, the elemental beings of earth. The gnomes can also tell you about the other earth signs, Taurus and Capricorn.

How to invoke the elemental beings is a book in itself and if you're interested in elemental magickal invocations, then I suggest you read *Magick of the Elements* (tentative title) by Richard Greene which is scheduled to be published in 1988. (My address is at the end of the book. If you are interested, you can write to me for details about this book.)

---

*There is a great deal of difference between magic and magick. Magic refers to sleight-of-hand tricks. Magick refers to spiritual practices that transform your consciousness.

_____ THREE FINAL COMMENTS

Three final comments for those readers who are astrology students. First, as you study astrology, be sure to keep in mind that the ability to learn astrology involves so much more than memorizing key words and key concepts. **Astrology is a system of reality that you must enter into in order to fully understand its meaning.** The more you understand it, the more it becomes a part of your personal worldview.

Second, because learning astrology is not the same as learning multiplication tables, **don't judge yourself and measure your progress against the progress of others.** Everyone develops their astrological understanding differently — according to their own personal awareness, their intuitive ability and their desire to learn.

Third, don't worry if you are unfamiliar with the various branches of astrology. Here again, let your intuition guide you to those astrological paths which are best for you. Your purpose with astrology may be as an astrological counselor, an economic forecaster or a skilled teacher. Or it may be that you will never become a professional astrologer but you will always use astrology as a personal aid. **No matter what path you choose, if you have followed your intuition then it is right for you. And that's all that matters.**

★━━━PART TWO

INVOKING THE FOUR ELEMENTS

★━━━━━━━━ CHAPTER FOUR

The Fire Element

FIRE SIGNS:

♈ ARIES (MARCH 21-APRIL 19)*

♌ LEO (JULY 23-AUGUST 22)*

♐ SAGITTARIUS (NOVEMBER 22-DECEMBER 21)*

*These dates will vary slightly from year to year.

MASCULINE, POSITIVE POLARITY: The fire signs are referred to as masculine or positive signs. This classification has nothing to do with gender nor does it indicate superiority. Instead, these terms refer to an outward, expressive nature.

FIRE ELEMENTALS: Magickal tradition states that every element has its own elemental beings that live in it. The fire elementals are lizard-like creatures called salamanders. Those of you who have studied the Tarot are probably familiar with them since they are pictured in various cards in the rod (fire) suit.

Before you begin the Fire Element Invocation, take note of how you feel mentally, emotionally and physically. Is your mind racing or calm? Are you feeling excited or upset? Is your body relaxed or tense? Write down your observations so you can compare your feelings after the Invocation.

MENTAL THOUGHTS _____

_____

_____

_____

_____

EMOTIONAL FEELINGS_____

_____

_____

_____

_____

PHYSICAL SENSATIONS _____

_____

_____

_____

_____

_____ **THE FIRE ELEMENT INVOCATION**

1. Begin by sitting or lying down in a comfortable position.

2. Imagine that you are surrounded by fire. Imagine that you can feel the fire's intense heat and warmth.

3. Keeping the image and sensation of a fire in your mind, now imagine that you are also surrounded by a bright red color. (Red is the color associated with the fire element.)

4. Imagine that this bright red color and the fire's heat are coming through the pores of your body and filling it up. See your whole body filled up with fire and the color red. Imagine that the sensation of heat is penetrating throughout your whole body.

5. Now that you have successfully imagined the red color and the heat as being outside and inside your body, try to maintain this image for 3-5 minutes.

6. Notice any feelings, emotions, physical sensations, thoughts or images that come to mind. Do you feel different than before you started the invocation? In what way?

7. At your own pace, leave the inner world of the fire element and open your eyes. When you are ready, move on to the next page.

While the memory of your trip into the fire element is still fresh, write down how you feel now. And then compare it with how you felt before you invoked the fire element.

MENTAL THOUGHTS _____
_____
_____
_____
_____

EMOTIONAL FEELINGS _____
_____
_____
_____
_____

PHYSICAL SENSATIONS_____
_____
_____
_____
_____

The following is a list of keywords associated with the fire element. As you read through this list, try to get an overall sense of fire's basic energy. Don't think that every quality listed below will apply to a person whose sun sign is in Aries, Leo or Sagittarius (the three fire signs). Not every fire sign is bossy, arrogant, unstable or abrupt!

Also, as you read the list below, don't make the mistake of thinking that these qualities only apply to individuals born under the fire signs. Of course this is not true! Keep in mind that these are only keywords for the fire element. Certainly, they do apply to people born while the sun was in Aries, Leo or Sagittarius. But your astrological personality is so much more than just your sun sign! Just to give one brief example, an individual born with his Sun in Scorpio, his Moon in Aries and his Mars in Sagittarius would be a very fiery individual, even though his sun is in the water sign Scorpio.

FIRE ELEMENT KEYWORDS LIST

Aggressive	Active	Expansive	Independent
Willful	Dynamic	Pioneering	Individualized
Initiator	Self-assured	Courageous	Inspirational
Ambitious	Go-getter	Confident	Experiential
Dominating	Powerful	Charismatic	Action-oriented
Outfront	Overbearing	Illuminating	Take-charge
Irresponsible	Catalyst	Showy	Freedom-loving
Sexual	Scattered	Volatile	Spontaneous
Violent	Impatient	High-spirited	Original
Daring	Energized	Outward	Creative
Pushy	Abrupt	External	Instinctual
Forceful	Demanding	Leadership	Exciting
Reactive	Explosive	Open	Passionate
Explorative	Bossy	Arrogant	Purifier
Territorial	Adventurous	Argumentative	Unstable
Competitive	Joyful	Conquering	Impulsive

Finally, compare your experience within the fire element to the Fire Element Keywords List. Write those keywords that best describe your journey into the fire element: _____

_____

_____

_____

_____ FIRE SIGNS: ARIES, LEO, SAGITTARIUS

Even though Aries, Leo and Sagittarius are all fire signs, this does not mean that they are exactly alike. Each fire sign emphasizes a different aspect of the fire element and this is expressed through their different symbols and glyphs. Read the brief descriptions below to get a better idea of their varied, fiery expressions.

ARIES: BORN FREE

Symbol: The Wild Ram
Glyph: ♈

As the first sign of the zodiac, Aries is the fearless and bold pioneer who instinctively pushes forward and discovers new territories. Like his symbol, the wild ram, who fearlessly attacks all obstacles with the power of his mighty horns, the ambitious, aggressive and sometimes argumentative Aries physically pushes his way forward.

Similar in nature to the wild ram who roams free, the undomesticated, independent Aries values his independence above anything else. Like an impatient young child, he wants his desires met immediately.

"Born free" is his motto, and he's determined to keep it that way. Even if his brash, independent, and sometimes arrogant nature overwhelms you and turns you off, you still have to admire his gutsy approach to life.

LEO: STAR OF THE DAY

Symbol: The Lion
Glyph: ♌

Feeling a strong kinship with his symbol, the "King of the Jungle" lion, the Leo feels aristocratic, no matter what his economic or social status truly is. Projecting confidence and self assurance, the royal Leo acts like a leader and people often assume he is. However, sometimes his royal power is all a show, as it is for the lion; the powerful king of the jungle does very little but eat and mate. It's the lioness who does all the work!

Leo is the zodiac's star performer who wants to experience and receive recognition for his individualistic creative energy. Carrying himself with celebrity stature, his personal charisma naturally draws attention and admiration. With a bigger-than-life attitude, his passion and zest for life contagiously light the sparks of joy and creativity in everyone he meets.

At his best, he is a child engrossed in play whose pleasure of life reminds you that life can be fun and, in the end, you are (and should be!) the star in your personal life drama.

SAGITTARIUS: LIFE SEEKER

Symbol: An Archer Centaur
Glyph: ♐

"Experiencing" is an important key word for all three fire signs, although what they seek to experience differs greatly. Where Aries wants to experience the potential of his will and his personal power, the Leo wants to experience his individuality and self creativity. In contrast is the Sagittarius who seeks to broaden and expand his activities and consciousness beyond the personal sphere. Inspired by dreams of greater possibilities, the Sagittarius is the eternal student, the international adventurer and the spiritual pilgrim in search of a greater awareness that transcends personal boundaries.

The Sagittarius's desire to go beyond personal reality is well expressed through his symbol, the mythological centaur. According to legend, the centaur was a creature whose body was half horse (lower body) and half human (upper body). As the symbol for Sagittarius, the centaur is always portrayed as an archer shooting his arrows up into the heavens. The upward direction of the arrow symbolizes Sagittarius's desire to reach for a higher consciousness and grasp a larger life perspective.

One interesting myth that symbolically reveals Sagittarius's higher aspirations concerns Chiron, the famous and wise centaur. When he died, Zeus placed him in the heavens in the Sagittarius constellation. Further emphasizing this drive for higher consciousness is Sagittarius's glyph — the centaur's arrow. Each Sagittarius, in his own way, seeks to understand life's greater meaning and, by no coincidence, Sagittarius is the sign associated with higher education, religion, travel, history, law, sociology and philosophy.

_____ **CHALLENGE YOURSELF**

   If you are already somewhat familiar with sun signs, this is a good opportunity to challenge yourself. Some of the words in the preceding Fire Element Keywords List describe all three fire signs. Other keywords are more appropriate for one or two fire signs.

   For example, *active* is a keyword that fits all three fire signs. *Pioneering* is an Aries keyword, *illuminating* is a Leo keyword and *inspirational* is a Sagittarius keyword. In my opinion the word *bossy* describes both Aries and Leo, but not Sagittarius.

   I'm purposely not going to go through the whole list and tell you what I think about each word. This is your time to listen to yourself. Treat this exercise as a game and don't worry about being right or wrong. Have fun!

   Fire Keywords That Fit All Three Signs: _____
_____
_____
_____
_____

   Aries Keywords: _____
_____
_____
_____
_____

   Leo Keywords: _____
_____
_____
_____
_____

   Sagittarius Keywords: _____
_____
_____
_____
_____

★ ■■■■■■■■■■■■■■■■ CHAPTER FIVE

The Water Element

WATER SIGNS:

♋ CANCER (JUNE 21-JULY 22)*

♏ SCORPIO (OCTOBER 23-NOVEMBER 21)*

♓ PISCES (FEBRUARY 19-MARCH 20)*

*These dates will vary slightly from year to year.

FEMININE, NEGATIVE POLARITY: The water signs are called the feminine or negative signs. Again, don't misconstrue the terms feminine and negative. Feminine does not refer to women and negative does not mean inferior. The water signs' feminine, negative classification refers to its inward, introspective orientation.

WATER ELEMENTALS: The traditional magickal water elementals are the mermaids and mermen. The upper halves of their bodies resemble a human body and their lower halves are fish tails. However, all water creatures belong to the water element and as such are water element symbols.

Before you begin the Water Element Invocation, take note of how you feel mentally, emotionally and physically. Is your mind racing with thoughts or calm? Are you feeling excited or upset? Is your body relaxed or tense? Write down your observations so you can compare your feelings after the invocation.

MENTAL THOUGHTS _____
_____
_____
_____
_____

EMOTIONAL FEELINGS_____
_____
_____
_____
_____

PHYSICAL SENSATIONS _____
_____
_____
_____
_____

_____ THE WATER ELEMENT INVOCATION

1. Begin by sitting or lying down in a comfortable position.

2. Imagine that you are swimming in an ocean. Dive down below the surface so that you are completely surrounded by water. Try to imagine, to the best of your ability, the feeling of water touching your whole body. Imagine that you can feel the water's fluidity and wetness.

3. Keeping the above image in mind, also imagine that you are surrounded by a dark blue color. (Dark blue is the color associated with the water element. If you'd like, you can imagine the ocean water as a dark blue color.)

4. Next, imagine that the dark blue color and the ocean water are coming through the pores of your body and filling it up. See your whole body filled up with the color dark blue and ocean water. Imagine that the sensations of wetness and fluidity are penetrating throughout your whole body.

5. Now that you have successfully imagined the dark blue color and the ocean water as being inside and outside your body, try to maintain this image for 3-5 minutes.

6. Notice any feelings, emotions, physical sensations, thoughts or images that come to mind. Do you feel different than before you started the invocation? In what way?

   While the memory of your trip into the water element is still strong, write down how you feel now. Then compare it with how you felt before you invoked the water element.

   MENTAL THOUGHTS _____

_____

_____

_____

_____

   EMOTIONAL FEELINGS_____

_____

_____

_____

_____

   PHYSICAL SENSATIONS _____

_____

_____

_____

_____

The following list contains the keywords for the water element. As you read through this list, just try to get an overall feeling for the water element's basic energy. Don't make the mistake of thinking that every quality listed below will apply to a person whose sun sign is Cancer, Scorpio or Pisces. Not only is each sign different, there are many different levels of awareness within each sign.

Remember also that people who are not born under the sun signs Cancer, Scorpio or Pisces may have these qualities as well. For example, an individual born with his Sun in Libra would be an air sign. And yet, if this same individual had his Moon and Jupiter in Cancer, he would have a very watery side to his personality.

WATER ELEMENT KEYWORDS LIST

Emotional	Hidden	Receptive	Magickal
Moody	Secretive	Passive	Psychic
Fluid	Elusive	Mellow	Clairvoyant
Flowing	Behind-the-scenes	Low-key	Clairsentient
Compassionate	Deepening	Healing	Visionary
Heart-sense	Contemplative	Soothing	Fantasy
Imaginative	Illusionary	Nurturing	Dreamy
Introspective	Elusive	Nourishing	Symbolic
Astral	Inward	Feeling	Subconscious
Visual	Invisible	Caring	Mysterious
Sensitive	Subterranean	Formless	Subjective
Personal	Underground	Yielding	Embryonic
Seed Awareness	Undercurrent	Sensual	Foundational
Dependency	Intangible	Subtle	Potential
Possessive	Internal	Magnetic	Preparatory
Clinging	Covert	Fragile	Regenerative
Protective	Concealing	Irrational	

Finally, compare your experience within the water element to the Water Element Keywords List. Write those keywords that best describe your journey into the water element: _____
_____
_____
_____

————WATER SIGNS: CANCER, SCORPIO, PISCES

The water signs Cancer, Scorpio and Pisces emphasize different sides of the water element. The following introductory descriptions of the three water signs illustrate some of the differences in their watery nature.

CANCER: THERE'S NO PLACE LIKE HOME

Symbol: The Crab
Glyph: ♋

Like his symbol the crab, the Cancer is a hidden, aquatic individual. (Remember, all the water signs have a hidden, secretive nature.) Immersed in a sea of psychic energy and activated feelings, he often feels like a sponge soaking up incredible amounts of astral energy.

When his life is filled with love and affection, the Cancer is an emotionally open and giving individual. However, when negative emotional driftwood enters into his personal environment, he scurries to safety. Like the crab who walks sideways, the Cancer prefers to avoid unpleasant situations, rather than confronting them directly. If the negative driftwood becomes too much for the sensitive Cancer to handle, he retreats into his shell like a crab. When his pain is overwhelming, he lives from a defensive posture — hiding under the protection of his shell.

The Cancer doesn't have to live the rest of his life in a shell, although at times he may feel that it's the only possible option available. In order to avoid future emotional wounds, the Cancer has to do two things. First, he has to use his natural psychic ability in order to perceive a situation's future potential. Second, he has to let go of his pain and his past negative experiences. This is easier said than done because like a crab with big claws, the Cancer tends to tenaciously hold onto all his past emotional experiences.

Finally, like a crab who carries its home on its back, the Cancer places a great deal of value on home and family security. Like Dorothy in The Wizard of Oz, the Cancer knows that there's no place like home. However, sometimes the Cancer forgets that home is a state of mind and desperately looks for inner security through external possessions or relationships. When this happens, the Cancer has to be reminded, like Dorothy was by the good witch Glinda, that he always had the inner power to return home. While his journey home won't come from just tapping magickal shoes and saying a chant, it will come from using and believing in his astral powers.

SCORPIO: THE LIFE AND DEATH DUET

**Symbols: The Scorpion, The Snake, The Phoenix and
        The Eagle
Glyph: ♏**

Unlike the other signs in the zodiac, Scorpio has a number of symbols that express the Scorpio's personality extremes. Every sign has negative and positive potentials, but it's here in Scorpio that the archetypes of evil and good battle for supremacy.

Representing the dark side of life is the nocturnal desert animal, the scorpion, who hides from sunlight and carries with him a poisonous stinger. Approaching life as a one shot deal, the scorpion Scorpio shrinks from the joys of life and challenges Death to a duel.

The middle level Scorpio strives for higher consciousness, but is still anchored to his dark side to some degree through his emotional and physical needs and desires. Learning to let go of his personality based desires is a hard lesson that every Scorpio eventually confronts. But hard as it may be, death is necessary so that a new, transformed consciousness may be born.

The snake and the phoenix appropriately represent this middle level Scorpio who is always in the throes of the death/rebirth process. From a physical standpoint, the snake's association with death and rebirth makes sense since he regularly sheds his skin and creates a new one. Like the snake, the mythological phoenix is also reborn, but in a more dramatic fashion. According to legend, the phoenix dies by fire and is reborn in his ashes.

From a mythological point of view, the snake is often character- ized as an animal who possesses knowledge of life's hidden myster- ies. Like the legendary snake, the snake Scorpio is also interested in exploring life's esoteric secrets. For some Scorpios this interest will bring them into the field of psychology where they can probe, analyze and dissect the underlying motivations of human behavior. For other Scorpios, it will bring them beyond psychology, into the world of parapsychology, astrology and the occult.

On his highest levels, the Scorpio is a spiritual warrior who seeks to uncover the very essence of life itself, and in the process of doing so, uncovers his own inner spiritual essence. This is the eagle Scorpio whose clear vision guides him to his inner spiritual center. With a purified inner nature, he soars above the joys and sorrows of human existence.

PISCES: DEEP SOUL FISHING

Symbol: Two Fish Connected By a Cord
Glyph: ♓

Out of all the water signs, only the Pisces's symbol is an aquatic animal that lives solely in water. (Cancer's aquatic crab can live in and out of the water; none of Scorpio's animals live in water.) What this symbolizes is that Pisces is the most watery sign of the zodiac.

Although all the water signs are imaginative and psychic (water characteristics), it is the Pisces, even more than Cancer and Scorpio, who lives in the deep, watery, astral realms. Elusive as a deep sea fish, the Pisces is often perceived as an individual wrapped in a cloak of mystery. Slippery as a fish, it's hard to get a handle on the Pisces. Just when you think you know him, the illusion fades and he slips through your grasp once again.

This "now you see me, now you don't" illusionary nature is characterized by his symbol and glyph, the two connected fish. It's as if one fish swims to the surface and makes an appearance, while the other fish swims to the ocean floor and remains unseen.

Pisces's duality is most apparent in his conflicting desires to help the world while at the same time retreating to a secluded hermitage. The sensitive and compassionate Pisces feels compelled to reach out from the depths of his soul to help those less fortunate. No matter what he is — a psychologist, a minister, a social worker, or a civic-minded volunteer (to name just a few possibilities) — he gives his caring help, knowing it can make a difference.

However, in reaching out to help those in need, the sensitive Pisces is pained by life's harsh realities. Like the Cancer, he is a psychic sponge and has to watch out for assuming other peoples' emotional distress. As much as he wants to help, his sensitive nature often needs to take time out and retire to the quiet solace of his soul.

Like his glyph which represents two fish tied together, yet swimming in opposite directions, the Pisces constantly "swims" in two opposite directions. On one hand he wishes to help the world and save those in trouble. On the other hand, he wishes to avoid the real world altogether. The swim is less exhausting when the Pisces uses his psychic ability to discriminate between worthwhile and worthless causes. Without psychic discrimination, the good-hearted, trusting Pisces can gullibly fall for any story — hook, line, and sinker.

_____ **CHALLENGE YOURSELF**

Once again, if you already have some background knowledge of the zodiac, take some extra time to go through the Water Element Keywords List and pick out those words which appropriately describe all three water signs. Then go over the list again and choose those words which specifically fit one or two signs.

For example, in my opinion, *moody* is a Cancer keyword, *regenerative* is a Scorpio keyword and *fantasy* is a Pisces keyword. The word *emotional* applies to all three water signs, while the word *possessive* describes Cancer and Scorpio more than Pisces.

Water Keywords That Fit All Three Signs: _____

_____
_____
_____
_____

Cancer Keywords: _____

_____
_____
_____
_____

Scorpio Keywords: _____

_____
_____
_____
_____

Pisces Keywords: _____

_____
_____
_____
_____

★ ■■■■■■■■■■■■■■■■■■■■ **CHAPTER SIX**

The Air Element

AIR SIGNS:

Ⅱ GEMINI (MAY 21-JUNE 20)*

♎ LIBRA (SEPTEMBER 23-OCTOBER 22)*

♒ AQUARIUS (JANUARY 20-FEBRUARY 18)*

*These dates will vary slightly from year to year.

MASCULINE, POSITIVE POLARITY: Like the fire signs, the air signs are also referred to as masculine and positive. Sociable and communicative by nature, their masculine classification symbolizes their extroverted nature.

AIR ELEMENTALS: The air elementals are the fairies, also called the sylphs. They are small winged creatures who fly through the air. All air creatures belong to the air element and as such are air element symbols.

Before you begin the Air Element Invocation, take note of how you feel mentally, emotionally and physically. Is your mind racing or is it calm? Are you feeling excited or upset? Is your body relaxed or tense? Write down your observations so you can compare your feelings after the Invocation.

MENTAL THOUGHTS _____

_____

_____

_____

_____

EMOTIONAL FEELINGS _____

_____

_____

_____

_____

PHYSICAL SENSATIONS _____

_____

_____

_____

_____

───────────THE AIR ELEMENT INVOCATION

1. Begin by sitting or lying down in a comfortable position.

2. Imagine that you are flying in the sky. As you soar through the air, feel your weightlessness. Imagine the feeling of air touching your whole body.

3. Keeping the above image in mind, also imagine that you are surrounded by a light blue color. (Light blue is the color associated with the air element. If you'd like, you can imagine that the sky is a clear, light blue color.)

4. Next, imagine that this light blue air is coming through the pores of your body and filling it up. See your whole body completely filled up with light blue air. Imagine that the sensations of space and lightness are penetrating throughout your whole body.

5. Now that you successfully imagined the light blue color and the air as being inside and outside your body, try to maintain this image for 3-5 minutes.

6. Notice any feelings, emotions, physical sensations, thoughts or images that come to mind. Do you feel different than before you started the invocation? In what way?

7. At your own pace, leave the inner world of the air element and open your eyes. When you are ready, move on to the next page.

While the memory of your trip into the air element is still fresh, write down how you feel now. Then compare it with how you felt before you invoked the air element.

MENTAL THOUGHTS _____
_____
_____
_____
_____

EMOTIONAL FEELINGS _____
_____
_____
_____
_____

PHYSICAL SENSATIONS _____
_____
_____
_____
_____

As you read the keywords listed below, try to get an overall feeling for the air element's basic nature. Here also, don't assume that every quality listed below will equally apply to a person whose sun sign is Gemini, Libra or Aquarius. Remember, not only is each sign different, there are many different levels of consciousness within each sign.

Also, keep in mind that individuals who do not have an air sun sign may have some of these airy qualities in their personality due to other planetary influences. For example, an individual born with his Sun in Capricorn would be classified as an earth sign. However, if this same individual has his Mars and Jupiter in Gemini, then he has a strong mentalized personality.

AIR ELEMENT KEYWORDS LIST

Mental	Scientific	Nonjudgmental	Talkative
Intellectual	Discriminating	Conversationalist	Unbiased
Rational	Critical	Opinionated	Loquacious
Logical	Skeptical	Noncommittal	Garrulous
Objective	Cerebral	Changeable	Glib
Analytical	Conceptual	Indecisive	Verbose
Evaluate	Factual	Flighty	Sociable
Integrative	Hypothetical	Communicative	Spacey
Synthesize	Questioning	Superficial	Articulate
Knowledgeable	Inquisitive	Dissipative	Verbal
Thoughtful	Ideas	Nervous	Telepathy
Conscious mind	Abstract	Scattered	Writing
Reasoning	Contrasting	Versatile	Literary
Aloof	Balancing	Flexibility	Storytelling
Impersonal	Classify	Adaptable	High-brow
Detached	Categorize	Mimic	Cultural
Disassociated	Assimilate	Imitative	Educational

Finally, compare your experience within the air element to the Air Element Keywords List. Write those keywords that best describe your journey into the air element: _____

_____

_____

_____ AIR SIGNS: GEMINI, LIBRA, AQUARIUS

The air signs Gemini, Libra and Aquarius emphasize different aspects of the air element. The following introductory descriptions of the three air signs illustrate some of the differences in their airy nature.

GEMINI: TWINS FOREVER

Symbol: The Twins
Glyph: ♊

Since his symbol is the twins, it's easy to understand why a Gemini is never alone. Once a Gemini friend, explaining her twin character to me said, "I always have two voices speaking. I can succeed in shutting one voice off, but I can never get both of them quiet at the same time."

Thinking about two things at the same time, Gemini is the eternal student with an endless thirst for knowledge. Learning is a priority for the Gemini who always has another book to read, another class to attend, another person to meet. His hyperactive mind is constantly working on overtime as it seeks out new pieces of information that will help him know himself and his personal environment.

In the end, the Gemini has to learn to slow down and take the time to integrate and assimilate his many different pieces of information. Otherwise, his twin-like mind will endlessly argue pro and con points of view, never making a firm decision.

LIBRA: BALANCING THE SCALES

Symbol: A Pair of Scales
Glyph: ♎

Poised at the midpoint of the zodiac, the sign Libra is positioned between an individual indentity and a social identity. Balancing these dual identities is a lifelong preoccupation for the Libra who wants, above all, a harmoniously ordered, conflict free life. Although Libra's reputation is that of an individual already balanced, actually the Libra is often unbalanced but striving, through a constant juggling act, to keep his life tranquil and serene.

According to Greek mythology, the scales are associated with Themis, the Greek goddess of justice. Not all Libras are judges and lawyers, but each Libra in his own way is fairminded. Always willing to hear both sides of an issue in order to reach a balanced perspective, the Libra is well known as a trustworthy mediator and counselor whose advice is fair and unbiased.

AQUARIUS: THE FUTURE VISIONARY

Symbol: The Water Bearer
Glyph: ♒

While the air element generally refers to the logical, conscious mind, the Aquarius has the capacity to transcend the conscious mind's limitations and develop a universal consciousness.

Two clues indicating Aquarius's higher mental faculties are its symbol, the water bearer, and its glyph, which could equally represent air waves or ocean waves. Water is the element associated with the unconscious mind and its inner astral powers. With water pouring into Aquarius's mental consciousness (thanks to the water bearer), the Aquarius opens up his mind to nonphysical reflections and perceives potential, future possibilities. When he combines his vision of a future world with his natural communication skill, he has the ability to successfully impart a message that grabs his audience's attention.

CHALLENGE YOURSELF

This exercise of word association is truly an air element exercise. Air loves to test its knowledge! As you did with the fire and water elements, give yourself a chance to see how much you already know. Read over the Air Element Keywords List. Pick out which words seem to fit all three air signs and which words seem most appropriate for Gemini, Libra or Aquarius.

To get you started, I'll give you a few ideas. In my opinion, *mimic* fits Gemini, *balancing* fits Libra, and *telepathy* fits Aquarius. Certainly *sociable* fits all three signs, while *scientific* is more descriptive of Gemini and Aquarius, not Libra.

Air Keywords That Fit All Three Signs: _____
_____
_____
_____
_____

Gemini Keywords: _____
_____
_____
_____
_____

Libra Keywords: _____
_____
_____
_____
_____

Aquarius Keywords: _____
_____
_____
_____
_____

★ ■■■■■■■■■■■■■■■■■■■■■■■ **CHAPTER SEVEN**

The Earth Element

EARTH SIGNS:

♉ TAURUS (APRIL 20-MAY 20)*

♍ VIRGO (AUGUST 23-SEPTEMBER 22)*

♑ CAPRICORN (DECEMBER 22-JANUARY 19)*

*These dates will vary slightly from year to year.

FEMININE, NEGATIVE POLARITY: Although not as introspective as the water signs, the earth signs also have a feminine, negative polarity that indicates an inner orientation.

EARTH ELEMENTALS: The traditional, magickal earth elementals are the gnomes, trolls, leprachauns and elves. However, all of earth's creatures are symbols of the earth element.

Before you begin the Earth Element Invocation, take note of how you feel mentally, emotionally and physically. Is your mind racing or is it calm? Are you feeling excited or upset? Is your body relaxed or tense? Write down your observations so you can compare your feelings after the Invocation.

MENTAL THOUGHTS _____

_____

_____

_____

_____

EMOTIONAL FEELINGS_____

_____

_____

_____

_____

PHYSICAL SENSATIONS _____

_____

_____

_____

_____

─────────THE EARTH ELEMENT INVOCATION

1. Begin by sitting or lying down in a comfortable position.

2. You can imagine that you are inside planet Earth or inside a big mountain. In any case, imagine that you are surrounded by compact, concentrated, heavy earth.

3. Keeping the above image in mind, also imagine that you are surrounded by a brown color. (Brown is the color associated with the earth element.)

4. Next, imagine that this brown color is coming through the pores of your body and filling it up. At the same time, imagine that your whole body is contracting and getting heavier.

5. Now that you have successfully imagined the brown color and imagined a sense of heaviness as being inside and outside your body, try to maintain this image for 3-5 minutes.

6. Notice any feelings, emotions, physical sensations, thoughts or images that come to mind. Do you feel different than before you started the invocation? In what way?

7. At your own pace, leave the inner world of the earth element and open your eyes. When you are ready, move on to the next page.

While the memory of your trip into the earth element is still fresh, write down how your feel now. Then compare it with how you felt before you invoked the earth element.

MENTAL THOUGHTS _____

_____

_____

_____

_____

EMOTIONAL FEELINGS _____

_____

_____

_____

_____

PHYSICAL SENSATIONS _____

_____

_____

_____

_____

The list below contains keywords which are descriptive of the earth element energy. As you read through this list, try to get an overall sense of earth's basic energy. The characteristics listed below are not meant to describe in full a person born under any of the three earth signs: Taurus, Virgo and Capricorn. Nor are they applicable to each and every earth sign.

Also keep in mind that an individual can have an earthy side to his personality even if his sun sign is not in Taurus, Virgo or Capricorn. For example, an individual with his Sun in Aries who also has Mercury, Venus and Mars in Taurus would have a very strong practical nature indeed!

EARTH ELEMENT KEYWORDS LIST

Practical	Reliable	Conservative	Permanent
Pragmatic	Dependable	Traditional	Stability
Realistic	Predictable	Cautious	Security
Commonsense	Enduring	Protective	Status quo
Down-to-earth	Durable	Careful	Materially-oriented
Serious	Persistent	Hesitant	Form
Purposeful	Perseverance	Reserved	Tangible
Usefulness	Steady	Inhibited	Consolidated
Utilitarian	Constant	Repressed	Solidified
Functional	Gradual	Rigid	Crystallized
Economical	Plodding	Inflexible	Organized
Productive	Thoroughness	Fixed	Structured
Work	Committed	Limited	Focused
Responsibility	Patient	Restricted	Defined
Duty	Sensual	Contracted	Ordered
Detailed	Mundane	Stagnant	Controlled

Finally, compare your experience within the earth element to the Earth Element Keywords List. Write those keywords that best describe your journey into the earth element: _____

_____

_____

_____

___ EARTH SIGNS: TAURUS, VIRGO, CAPRICORN

The three earth signs – Taurus, Virgo and Capricorn – emphasize and express different aspects of the earth element. The following introductory descriptions of the three earth signs illustrate some of the differences in their earth nature.

TAURUS: THE NATURE LOVER

Symbol: The Bull
Glyph: ♉

When the grass is green and the fragrance of blossoming flowers is everywhere in the air, you can be sure that the sign Taurus has finally arrived. Born in the middle of spring, is it any wonder that Taurus is the nature child of the zodiac?

Even more than the other earth signs Virgo and Capricorn, the Taurus is an individual who needs communion with nature to revitalize his inner spirit. Not surprisingly, many a Taurus is attracted to gardening and his love of nature often gives him that extra touch – the green thumb!

Symbolizing the Taurus's deep connection with nature is the bull, an ancient religious fertility symbol. My favorite bull legend, which clearly demonstrates the bull's fertility powers, comes from the Persian Mithraic religion. According to the legend, Mithra had to kill his companion, the Heavenly Bull, so that humankind would prosper. Sure enough, once the bull died, all plant life grew out of its body and multiplied throughout the world. Even animals such as the cow, the horse and the camel, who are helpful to humankind, were born from the bull's remains.

The bull is a domesticated animal and its connection to other domesticated animals in the Mithraic myth gives us an important clue regarding the Taurus's character. Unlike its previous sign — the wild, undomesticated Aries – the Taurus seeks a stable, domesticated life. While Aries is the adventurous trailblazer, Taurus is the homesteader who settles down. Once he has put down his roots, the bullheaded Taurus hates to change. Like a tree that stays in one place and slowly branches out from its trunk, the Taurus needs a secure, dependable base before he too branches out.

VIRGO: LIKE A VIRGIN

Symbol: A Virgin
Glyph: ♍

Virgo is the sign of self perfection and the Virgo works hard to eliminate any imperfections that arise. Like his symbol, the virgin, the Virgo strives for purity in thought, word and deed.

This drive for purity is mythologically expressed by the goddess Astrea, the goddess of innocence and purity. According to legend, Astrea lived on earth until the Iron Age, when humankind became wicked. It was during this time that all the gods left earth, including innocent Astrea, who could not maintain her presence in the midst of such evil. Leaving earth, she took up residence in the sky as the Virgo constellation.

Desiring self perfection on the physical level, the virginal Virgo is a health conscious individual who knows the importance of eating nutritious food and exercising regularly. Whether he's a vegetarian or a meat eater, a marathon runner or a skier, the Virgo wants to keep his body in good shape (preferably, perfect shape).

On a mental level, the Virgo is often drawn to psychology (and sometimes astrology) in order to better understand his mind. Mental self improvement is part of his personal discipline as he seeks to resolve inner conflicts and eradicate bad negative habits, insecurities and fears.

Operating on a positive level, the virginal Virgo seeks to become independent and self reliant, like the mythological virgin goddesses.

The symbol of the virgin for the sign Virgo does not apply to this sign's sexual status, but instead indicates a clear, inner attitude. Like the unmarried virgin goddesses who are complete unto themselves, the Virgo seeks to be a complete, actualized individual.

The Virgo who fails to understand that purity is a state of mind, thinks that self perfection can be created through regimented, controlling behavior. It's as if he lives under the shadow of the virgin woman Pandora who unleased physical and mental illness on the world when she opened the forbidden box (now called Pandora's box). Fearful of unleashing his personal demons, the Virgo represses his feelings and mistakenly equates self protection with self perfection. Sadly, this type of Virgo is more akin to a lifeless mannequin than a vibrant goddess.

CAPRICORN: THE STRATEGIC PLANNER

Symbols: The Mountain Goat and The Sea-Goat
Glyph: ♑

The strategic planner of the zodiac, the Capricorn has an excellent, organizational, executive mind which can be understood through the symbol, the mountain goat.

Like the goat who has reached the mountain top and can see for miles around, the Capricorn is able to objectively see the big picture without getting bogged down by small details (like a Virgo might do). Able to perceive and clarify the larger purpose of the issues at hand, the Capricorn capably creates effective, long term strategies.

Once his purpose is determined and his plans are finalized, the Capricorn begins his long climb to success. Just as the mountain goat slowly but surely climbs to the mountain top, the Capricorn steadily advances toward his goal. With the purpose of his objective and the patience of a mountain goat, nothing will deter him from accomplishing his dream.

The Capricorn's dogged determination brings to mind Aesop's fable, "The Tortoise and The Hare." Although the tortoise's win seemed unlikely at first, the tortoise capitalized on the hare's inconsistent behavior and won the race through his own consistent efforts. Like the tortoise, the Capricorn gets ahead and finds success by staying on course and focusing on his goal.

At first glance the ancient Capricorn symbol, the mythological sea-goat (a goat with a fish tail), might seem completely inappropriate. After all, what symbolizes the ambitious, goal-oriented Capricorn better than the mountain goat who climbs to the mountain top and surveys all that he has accomplished!

However, I think the sea-goat has its place in this sign and actually represents an evolved Capricornian awareness. Consider this: nothing can materialize in the physical world unless it has first been imagined. The mythological sea-goat symbolically illustrates this connection between the earthy, physical plane (the goat half) and the watery, astral plane (the fish tail). Understanding that material success and the power of imagination (a water keyword) go hand in hand, the sea-goat Capricorn consciously uses his inner, visionary power as he formulates his goals and implements his strategies.

CHALLENGE YOURSELF

One last time! Read over the Earth Element Keywords List again and write down those words which seem to equally describe all three earth signs. Then go back and pick out those words which are more in tune with a specific sign or two signs.

For example, *sensual* is a Taurus keyword, *detailed* is a Virgo keyword and *contracted* is a Capricorn keyword. *Practical* is a word that equally describes all three earth signs, while *ordered* is a word that better describes Virgo and Capricorn, not Taurus.

Earth Keywords That Fit All Three Signs: _____
_____
_____
_____
_____

Taurus Keywords: _____
_____
_____
_____
_____

Virgo Keywords: _____
_____
_____
_____
_____

Capricorn Keywords: _____
_____
_____
_____
_____

★ ▬▬PART THREE

LEARNING THE ELEMENTAL LANGUAGE

★ ══════════════════ CHAPTER EIGHT

Playing With The Elements

As with the study of any new language, at first the goal of fluency may appear to be an insurmountable, impossible task. This is because when you first begin to learn a new language, you have not assimilated the words on your inner, unconscious levels. In other words, your unconscious mind has not yet connected images, feelings and emotions to the new information that your conscious mind is trying to memorize and categorize. Without an inner connection to the astrological language through his unconscious mind, it is no wonder that the beginning astrology student perceives astrology as a body of knowledge exterior to his own personal reality. As much as the beginner may already believe in astrology, until inner assimilation of the language takes place, astrology is seen and experienced as something existing outside of himself.

The key to advancing in your facility with the astrological language lies in your ability and determination to utilize your personal power to assimilate your astrological knowledge on the deeper levels of your consciousness. When you begin to assimilate the astrological language, you are actually using your personal power to bring meaning to the outer framework of astrology. As assimilation occurs, words begin to have feelings and images behind them and when this happens, you begin to *own* the meaning behind the words. When this occurs, the outer astrological framework is transformed into an inner perception of reality that literally changes the way you see the world. While the beginning student sees astrology as outside of himself, the advanced student experiences astrology as an inner framework that colors his life perceptions.

For those impatient students who are just beginning to study astrology, please remember that people don't become fluent overnight in any language and astrology is no exception. By fluent I don't mean the ability to recite all the names of the signs and their corresponding elements. Instead, astrological fluency is the ability to enter into the symbolic, astral world that is behind the astrological language. In other words, an astrologically fluent individual is someone who can easily feel, sense and clearly communicate the meaning of a particular sign, planet, house, aspect or chart.

Like an infant who is learning language by playing with sounds and voice inflections, it is important for an astrology student to **play** with his or her own level of astrological knowledge. How quickly you learn and become astrologically fluent depends on how open you are and how persistent you are in using your present astrological language and applying it to different aspects of life.

The purpose of this chapter is to give you the opportunity to play with your elemental knowledge. You will play at being fire, water, air, and earth and seeing different aspects of life through their individual elemental eyes.

As you play with each exercise, if you have trouble with any element, don't give up. Simply take the time to invoke the element and then continue on with the exercise.

Finally, as you go through each exercise, I suggest you play first and then afterwards turn to the appendix at the end of the book to see some additional answers. Don't worry if you come up with something different — there are many answers.

Also, don't make the mistake of thinking that once you've done the exercise, there's no point going over it again. Remember, there's a multitude of answers waiting to be discovered by you and new insights will continue to emerge as you become more fluent. I've been studying astrology for a very long time and I'm still learning.

So, enough of these philosophical musings, it's time to **play** with the four elements!

_____THE ELEMENTS' PHYSICAL FORMS

In this exercise, imagine the different ways that the four elements manifest on the physical plane. To get you started, I've listed a few ways in which the elements materialize. Imagine other ways the elements are manifested and add them to the list below.

FIRE: Campfire, fire in a fireplace _____

_____

_____

_____

_____

WATER: An ocean, a rainstorm _____

_____

_____

_____

_____

AIR: Blue sky, wind currents _____

_____

_____

_____

_____

EARTH: Topsoil, mountains, metal _____

_____

_____

_____

————————————— PHYSICAL INTERACTIONS

In the previous exercise you imagined the different physical expressions of each element. Now in this exercise, expand your imagination to see how each element could be affected by the other remaining three elements.

For example, how is fire affected by water? To find the answer to this question, let your mind imagine a scenario where the water element is interacting with the fire element. For example, you could begin by imagining the fire element as a campfire. The water element could be represented by a rainstorm. What happens to the campfire when it rains? If the rain is heavy, the fire will go out. However, if it's just a light drizzle, the fire will remain but be smaller. Just from this one example, you can see that judging from its physical effect, the water element has the capacity to reduce fire or even destroy fire altogether.

As you go through this exercise, feel free to refer to the previous page. Let your mind imagine more than just one scenario. As we saw in the campfire example above, if you vary the strength of an element (as we did with the water element), the outcome of the elemental interactions will vary.

To get you started on this exercise, I've filled in the first section using the campfire and rainstorm scenario.

1. How Is Fire Affected By:

a. **Water?**
   Scenario: A campfire rained out by a heavy rainstorm.
   Result: Water can destroy fire.

b. **Air?**
   Scenario: _____

Result: _____

_____

c. **Earth?**
   Scenario: _____

   _____

   Result: _____

   _____

2. How Is Water Affected By:

a. **Fire?**
   Scenario: _____

   Result: _____

   _____

b. **Air?**
   Scenario: _____

   Result: _____

   _____

c. **Earth?**
   Scenario: _____

   Result: _____

   _____

3. How is Air Affected By:

a. Fire?
   Scenario: _____

   _____

   Result: _____

   _____

b. Water?
   Scenario: _____

   _____

   Result: _____

   _____

c. Earth?
   Scenario: _____

   _____

   Result: _____

   _____

4. How Is Earth Affected By:

a. Fire?
   Scenario: _____

   _____

   Result: _____

   _____

b. Water?
  Scenario: _____

  _____

  Result: _____

  _____

c. Air?
  Scenario: _____

  _____

  Result: _____

  _____

──────────ELEMENTAL CONVERSATIONS FROM A PHYSICAL PERSPECTIVE

Now, let your imagination empower the elements with the gift of speech and, based on their physical interactions in the previous exercise, create an imaginary conversation between the elements.

For example, in response to the heavy rainstorm, the fire element might say, "You put out my fire!" Or in response to a light drizzling rain, fire might say, "You really dampen my spirit!" Both these sayings, by the way, are typical reactions of fire sign individuals (Aries, Leo, Sagittarius) to water sign individuals (Cancer, Scorpio, Pisces). These two elements and the natives born under the fire and water signs are simply very different in nature — which is obvious from their physical reactions.

If you find yourself unable to imagine a conversation, then simply put yourself in the shoes of the element that is being affected. For example, in the campfire/rainstorm scenario, first imagine yourself as a campfire that is burning brightly and enjoy the heat and the light of the flames. Next, imagine raindrops falling on you (the campfire). How do you feel? Do you welcome the rain or cringe at its touch? Experience the campfire's reactions; don't just intellectualize about them.

1. What Would Fire Say To:

a. Water? _____

_____

_____

_____

b. Air? _____

_____

_____

_____

c. Earth? _____

_____

_____

_____

2. What Would Water Say To:

a. Fire? _____

_____

_____

_____

b. Air? _____

_____

_____

_____

c. Earth? _____

_____

_____

_____

3. What Would Air Say To:

a. Fire? _____

_____

_____

_____

b. Water? _____

_____

_____

_____

c. Earth? _____

_____

_____

_____

4. What Would Earth Say To:

a. Fire? _____

_____

_____

_____

b. Water? _____

_____

_____

_____

c. Air? _____

_____

_____

_____

────────THE ELEMENTS' PSYCHOLOGICAL EXPRESSIONS

As you saw in the keyword lists in the Part Two, each element is associated with different mental and emotional attitudes. In this exercise, I want you to try to write down the different psychological expressions for each element. If you get stuck, go back to the keyword lists. But first, give yourself the opportunity to see how much you already know. I've given you a few keywords to get you going.

FIRE: Impulsive, passionate, freedom-loving, _____

_____

_____

_____

_____

WATER: Emotional, sensitive, caring, _____

_____

_____

_____

_____

AIR: Intellectual, communicative, objective, _____

_____

_____

_____

_____

EARTH: Practical, consistent, productive, _____

_____

_____

_____

_____

─────────PSYCHOLOGICAL INTERACTIONS

Now that you have explored the individual psychological ap-proaches of each element, it is time to consider how the elements might interact with each other. Just as you can consider the physical interactions of the element, so too can you also examine their psychological interactions.

Here again, let's examine how fire would be affected by water, from a psychological perspective. For our purposes, let's play with a few fire and water psychological keywords. On one hand, fire can be a charismatic element. Influenced by water, an element associated with emotions, this could indicate a very powerful combination. A person with this fire/water contact of this nature, could be in touch with other peoples' emotions and use that understanding, along with the fiery charisma, to lead and influence people.

On the other hand, if you look at more negative fire characteris-tics, such as volatility or explosiveness and combine them with the emotional sensitivity of water, you could get a very unpredictable and emotionally unstable individual.

As you did with the Physical Interaction Exercise, feel free to refer to the previous page or the keyword list in Chapters 4-7. Here again, let your mind consider more than just one scenario. Remember, there are always positive and negative traits for all the elements and depending on how you combine the elements, you can come up with some very different types of psychological combination. Have fun playing with the different possibilities!

1. How Is Fire Affected By:

a. Water?
Keywords: Volatility (fire)/Emotional sensitivity (water)
Result: Emotional unpredictability, moodiness
Keywords: _____
Result: _____
Keywords: _____
Result: _____

b. Air?
Keywords: _____
Result: _____
Keywords: _____
Result: _____
Keywords: _____
Result: _____

c. Earth?
Keywords: _____
Result: _____
Keywords: _____
Result: _____
Keywords: _____
Result: _____

2. How is Water Affected By:

a. **Fire?**
   Keywords: _____
   Result: _____
   Keywords: _____
   Result: _____
   Keywords: _____
   Result: _____

b. **Air?**
   Keywords: _____
   Result: _____
   Keywords: _____
   Result: _____
   Keywords: _____
   Result: _____

c. **Earth?**
   Keywords: _____
   Result: _____
   Keywords: _____
   Result: _____
   Keywords: _____
   Result: _____

3. How Is Air Affected By:

a. Fire?
Keywords: _____
Result: _____
Keywords: _____
Result: _____
Keywords: _____
Result: _____

b. Water?
Keywords: _____
Result: _____
Keywords: _____
Result: _____
Keywords: _____
Result: _____

c. Earth?
Keywords: _____
Result: _____
Keywords: _____
Result: _____
Keywords: _____
Result: _____

4. How Is Earth Affected By:

a. Fire?
Keywords: _____

Result: _____

Keywords: _____

Result: _____

Keywords: _____

Result: _____

b. Water?
Keywords: _____

Result: _____

Keywords: _____

Result: _____

Keywords: _____

Result: _____

c. Air?
Keywords: _____

Result: _____

Keywords: _____

Result: _____

Keywords: _____

Result: _____

_____ELEMENTAL CONVERSATIONS FROM A PSYCHOLOGICAL PERSPECTIVE

Now that you have richly endowed the elements with feelings, emotions, and motivations, imagine them as they would converse with each other.

For example, what would spirited and carefree fire say if it met water during one of her fits of moodiness? Most likely fire would say something like, "Stop wallowing in your misery and go out and DO something!"

Or to give another example, what would cautious earth say to the ivory-towered, intellectual air? Probably something like, "Practical on-the-job experience is worth more than the knowledge of a dozen degrees!"

As we have seen earlier, each element has positive and negative traits. What conversations emerge between the elements will depend on which traits the elements are expressing. For example, air can be an airhead or an intellectual giant while fire can be an enthusiastic, charismatic leader or an angry, impatient child. Likewise, water can be an extremely psychic individual or an ultrasensitive individual whose feelings are hurt by the slightest comment. And finally, earth can be a shrewd, business person or a boring stick-in-the-mud.

As you do the next exercise, keep the diversity of each element in mind. Begin by picking elemental keywords and then go on to construct a two-way conversation. The conversations you create will depend on what aspect of the elements you choose. Read my two examples of fire-water dialogue and you'll get an idea of what I mean.

1. FIRE TO WATER

Fire Keyword: Upfront emotions
Water Keyword: Sensitive emotional nature
Fire's Comment: " Well, it's too bad if you don't like it, that's the way I feel!"

Water's Response: "Well you don't have to be so mean about it! Your angry words hurt me!"

Fire Keyword: Individualism
Water Keyword: Nurturing
Fire's Comment: " I have to make my mark on life and I have to do it my way!"
Water's Response: "I'm sure you'll be a tremendous success. I believe in you."

Fire Keyword: _____
Water Keyword: _____
Fire's Comment: _____
_____
Water's Response: _____
_____

2.   FIRE TO AIR

Fire Keyword: _____
Air Keyword: _____
Fire's Comment: _____
_____
Air's Response: _____
_____

Fire Keyword: _____
Air Keyword: _____
Fire's Comment: _____
_____
Air's Response: _____
_____

Fire Keyword: _____

Air Keyword: _____

Fire's Comment: _____

_____

Air's Response: _____

_____

3.   FIRE TO EARTH

Fire Keyword: _____

Earth Keyword: _____

Fire's Comment: _____

_____

Earth's Response: _____

_____

Fire Keyword: _____

Earth Keyword: _____

Fire's Comment: _____

_____

Earth's Response: _____

_____

Fire Keyword: _____

Earth Keyword: _____

Fire's Comment: _____

_____

Earth's Response: _____

_____

4. WATER TO FIRE

Water Keyword: _____

Fire Keyword: _____

Water's Comment: _____

_____

Fire's Response: _____

_____

Water Keyword: _____

Fire Keyword: _____

Water's Comment: _____

_____

Fire's Response: _____

_____

Water Keyword: _____

Fire Keyword: _____

Water's Comment: _____

_____

Fire's Response: _____

_____

5. WATER TO AIR

Water Keyword: _____

Air Keyword: _____

Water's Comment: _____

_____

Air's Response: _____

_____

Water Keyword: _____

Air Keyword: _____

Water's Comment: _____

_____

Air's Response: _____

_____

Water Keyword: _____

Air Keyword: _____

Water's Comment: _____

_____

Air's Response: _____

_____

6. WATER TO EARTH

Water Keyword: _____

Earth Keyword: _____

Water's Comment: _____

_____

Earth's Response: _____

_____

Water Keyword: _____

Earth Keyword: _____

Water's Comment: _____

_____

Earth's Response: _____

_____

Water Keyword: _____

Earth Keyword: _____

Water's Comment: _____

_____

Earth's Response: _____

_____

7. AIR TO FIRE

Air Keyword: _____

Fire Keyword: _____

Air's Comment: _____

_____

Fire's Response: _____

_____

Air Keyword: _____

Fire Keyword: _____

Air's Comment: _____

_____

Fire's Response: _____

_____

Air Keyword: _____

Fire Keyword: _____

Air's Comment: _____

_____

Fire's Response: _____

_____

8. AIR TO WATER

Air Keyword: _____

Water Keyword: _____

Air's Comment: _____

_____

Water's Response: _____

_____

Air Keyword: _____

Water Keyword: _____

Air's Comment: _____

_____

Water's Response: _____

_____

Air Keyword: _____

Water Keyword: _____

Air's Comment: _____

_____

Water's Response: _____

_____

9. AIR TO EARTH

Air Keyword: _____

Earth Keyword: _____

Air's Comment: _____

_____

Earth's Response: _____

_____

Air Keyword: _____

Earth Keyword: _____

Air's Comment: _____

_____

Earth's Response: _____

_____

Air Keyword: _____

Earth Keyword: _____

Air's Comment: _____

_____

Earth's Response: _____

_____

10. EARTH TO FIRE

Earth Keyword: _____

Fire Keyword: _____

Earth's Comment: _____

_____

Fire's Response: _____

_____

Earth Keyword: _____

Fire Keyword: _____

Earth's Comment: _____

_____

Fire's Response: _____

_____

Earth Keyword: _____

Fire Keyword: _____

Earth's Comment: _____
_____

Fire's Response: _____
_____

11. EARTH TO WATER

Earth Keyword: _____

Water Keyword: _____

Earth's Comment: _____
_____

Water's Response: _____
_____

Earth Keyword: _____

Water Keyword: _____

Earth's Comment: _____
_____

Water's Response: _____
_____

Earth Keyword: _____

Water Keyword: _____

Earth's Comment: _____
_____

Water's Response: _____
_____

12. EARTH TO AIR

Earth Keyword: _____

Air Keyword: _____

Earth's Comment: _____

_____

Air's Response: _____

_____

Earth Keyword: _____

Air Keyword: _____

Earth's Comment: _____

_____

Air's Response: _____

_____

Earth Keyword: _____

Air Keyword: _____

Earth's Comment: _____

_____

Air's Response: _____

_____

_____OTHER SUGGESTED PLAY ACTIVITIES

By now you should have a solid understanding of how the elements express themselves and how they interact with each other. But don't stop here. Even though you've finished this chapter, continue to challenge yourself to see the elements in action in everyday life. For example, if your boss wants you to prove the bottom-line impact of your new proposal, what element is he? Results-oriented, financially concerned earth, of course! And if your child is crawling all over the house, what element is he? Action-oriented fire! Absolutely everything in life can be perceived as an expression of the elements.

The questions I've listed below are just a few more ways to challenge your elemental knowledge. If you have some astrologically-minded friends, get together to go over the questions. The ideal situation is to have groups of four people so that each person in a group can play at being one of the elements. As you go through the different questions (along with any others you want to add on your own), switch elements so that everyone has an equal chance to experience all the elements. After everyone has stated their elemental point of view, engage in a give-and-take discussion. Disagree or agree with the other elements in a way that is appropriate for your element's perspective.

If you are doing this exercise by yourself, answer each question from the viewpoints of all four elements. I've given you a beginning clue for each question — have fun!

1. What do you consider fun?
   (The air element loves to read.)

2. What do you worry about?
   (The earth element worries about financial security.)

3. How do you feel about money?
   (The fire element wants money so he can have freedom to do what he wants.)

4. What qualities should your marriage partner have?
   (The water element wants someone who will care
   about her feelings.)

5. How would you react if you were unhappy with your job?
   (The fire element would go get another job!)

6. Think of famous proverbs and cliches and classify them by
   element.
   ("Haste makes waste" is definitely a cautious earth
   element saying!)

7. List different sports according to elements.
   (Swimming is a water sport.)

★ ■■■■■■■■■■■■■■■■■ **CHAPTER NINE**

The Planets From An Elemental Perspective

By studying the four elements in the previous chapters you already understand a great deal about the twelve signs and their inner motivations. However, while the four elements are the foundational cornerstones of the zodiac, the ruling planets and the three qualities are additional clues that unlock each sign's unique character.

In this chapter and the next chapter you will learn about the planets and the qualities, their connections to the elements and their use as clues to determine the focus of a sign beyond its basic elemental character.

■■■■■ CLUES TO A PLANET'S ELEMENTAL MAKEUP

Like the signs, the planets can be understood from an elemental perspective. One of the clues to a planet's elemental association is the elemental makeup of the sign it rules.

For those readers who are just beginning to study astrology, let me explain a little about the concept of a ruling planet. Every sign has a ruling planet. When a planet is said to rule a particular sign, this implies that the concerns of the planet and the sign it rules are very similar.

For example, Aries is a fire sign well known for its hot temper, impulsive actions and strong sexual drive. Not surprisingly, its ruling planet Mars is also associated with spontaneous actions, anger and sex. Since there is such a strong similarity between a sign and its ruling planet, it is logical to make an elemental connection between the planet and the sign it rules.

Simply put, when a planet rules a particular sign, then it also shares that sign's elemental orientation. Consequently, since Aries is a fire sign it follows that Mars, its ruling planet, must also be a fire planet.

Listed below are the signs, their ruling planets and their elemental associations.

SIGN	RULING PLANET	ELEMENT
Aries	Mars	Fire
Taurus	Venus	Earth
Gemini	Mercury	Air
Cancer	Moon	Water
Leo	Sun	Fire
Virgo	Mercury	Earth
Libra	Venus	Air
Scorpio	Pluto	Water
Sagittarius	Jupiter	Fire
Capricorn	Saturn	Earth
Aquarius	Uranus	Air
Pisces	Neptune	Water

It's also helpful to list the planets by their elemental classifications as I have done below.

FIRE	WATER	AIR	EARTH
Mars	Moon	Mercury	Venus
Sun	Pluto	Venus	Mercury
Jupiter	Neptune	Uranus	Saturn

You may have noticed that Mercury and Venus are associated with the air and the earth elements. Mercury rules Gemini (air) and Virgo (earth); Venus rules Taurus (earth) and Libra (air).

There's a simple reason for this. While there are twelve signs in the zodiac, astrologers only use the eight planets already discovered by astronomers and the sun and the moon. Filling in this gap, Mercury and Venus are the "planetary pinch hitters" of the zodiac, helping out, so to speak, until the true ruling planets of Virgo and Taurus are discovered.

Although Mercury and Venus are adequate in their rulership of Virgo and Taurus, they are unable to completely express the total potential of these two signs. Even so, by studying their planetary characteristics, you can still learn a great deal about Virgo and Taurus.

By the way, the idea of planets "pinch hitting" as planetary rulers is nothing new. Mars, Jupiter and Saturn each ruled two signs before Pluto, Neptune and Uranus were discovered.

BEFORE:

RULING PLANET	ZODIAC SIGNS
Mars	Aries and Scorpio
Jupiter	Sagittarius and Pisces
Saturn	Capricorn and Aquarius

NOW:

RULING PLANET	ZODIAC SIGN
Mars	Aries
Pluto	Scorpio
Jupiter	Sagittarius
Neptune	Pisces
Saturn	Capricorn
Uranus	Aquarius

Some astrologers accept the new ruling planets listed above, but believe that the old ruling planets are still in effect. In other words, they believe that Scorpio is co-ruled by Mars and Pluto, Pisces is co-ruled by Jupiter and Neptune and Aquarius is co-ruled by Saturn and Uranus. While I think it is important to recognize how the former ruling planets were appropriate in the past, I strongly feel that it's time to let go of the outdated rulerships and recognize that the new ruling planets stand by themselves as the most complete expressions of their respective signs.

For example, due to Mars's association with will, power and sex, it is appropriate that Mars once ruled Aries and Scorpio — the two power signs of the zodiac. However, Mars is a fire planet that burns out easily. In addition, remember how easily fire is put out by water (Scorpio is a water sign). Only Pluto, the true planetary ruler of Scorpio, has the concentrated, emotional intensity and depth that is Scorpio's trademark. I should know — I'm a Scorpio.

Likewise, before Neptune's discovery, it made sense that Jupiter, the planet of religion, ruled Sagittarius and Pisces, the two spiritually oriented signs.   However, while Jupiter's traditional, exoteric religious consciousness is at home in Sagittarius, the sign of established faith, it does not fully express Pisces's inner spiritual yearnings.   Only mystical Neptune rules the esoteric Pisces who transcends dogmatic religious teachings to embrace the spiritual unity in life.

Before Uranus's discovery in the late 1700's, society was organized according to rigid and inflexible religious and secular organizations. Consequently, it made sense that Saturn, the planet of traditional, hierarchical societal organization ruled both Capricorn and Aquarius, two signs concerned with society's organizations. However, once the democratic, humanitarian Uranus was discovered, the whole structure of society was challenged by the American and French revolutions. From the events surrounding its discovery, it became apparent that Uranus was the planet associated with revolutionaries and reformers. Saturn, the planet of the political establishment, could not possibly rule Aquarius. Only Uranus fits as the ruling planet of Aquarius, a sign well known for its socially concerned, humanitarian nature. The times have changed and so have the ruling planets.

—————PLANETARY CLUES TO THE DIFFERENCES IN THE ELEMENTAL TRIPLICITIES

Signs that share the same element are similar in nature and experience a strong affinity. For example, the three signs of the fire triplicity — Aries, Leo and Sagittarius — are well known for their independent, freedom-loving approach to life.

While their common fire elemental bond tells us much about these signs' similarities, profound differences in their fiery personalities remain that cannot be explained by their primary elemental makeup. For example, as you saw in Chapter Four, the fire signs express their individuality in three distinct ways. Aries is the curious child/pioneer, Leo is the showy/individualistic star, and Sagittarius is the optimistic teacher/philosopher.

Knowing that the fire element is a clue to the fire signs' similarities, the natural question to ask is "What are the clues to the fire signs' dissimilarities?"

Answer: The planetary rulers are major clues to understanding the fire signs' separate and unique personalities.

Indeed, as with the fire signs, the differences that exist between the signs in each elemental triplicity can be determined by understanding the signs' ruling planets.

It is not within the scope of this book to give you an in-depth explanation of the planets — that remains for future books. However, just by knowing some of the planetary keywords listed below, you'll begin to get a sense of the differences that exist in the signs that comprise an elemental triplicity.

———— FIRE TRIPLICITY: ARIES, LEO, SAGITTARIUS

Keywords for Mars — planetary ruler of Aries

> Instinctual will
> Primal consciousness
> Impulsive, spontaneous action
> Anger, aggression, assertiveness
> Vitality, sexual energy and physical energy

Keywords for the Sun — planetary ruler of Leo

> Self-directed will
> Ego consciousness, self awareness
> Self creativity
> Personality energy

Keywords for Jupiter — planetary ruler of Sagittarius

Reflective, spiritual will
Group consciousness, social awareness
Philosophy, optimism, education, culture
Higher knowledge, religion, morality
Socialized energy

Considering their planetary rulers, is it any wonder that Aries is the aggressive pioneer, Leo is the creative, charismatic individual and Sagittarius is the wise one who reflects upon the meaning of life? All three signs are fire signs but the differences are obvious when you consider their ruling planets.

— WATER TRIPLICITY: CANCER, SCORPIO, PISCES

Keywords for the Moon — planetary ruler of Cancer

Emotions, subconscious feelings
Psychic awareness
Family, home
Mother, motherhood

Keywords for Pluto — planetary ruler of Scorpio

Inner, transformational power
Inner sexual consciousness
Death and rebirth
Secrets and taboos
Hidden mysteries - the Occult
Emotional obsessions

Keywords for Neptune — planetary ruler of Pisces

> Unconscious emotions and fears
> Unconscious mind
> Psychic sensitivity, mediumship
> Spiritual, soul awareness
> Spiritually inspired creativity
> Fantasy, vivid imagination
> Illusion, deceit

Try to feel the energies behind these planetary keywords and then apply it to the corresponding signs. For example, all three signs are emotionally oriented, but Cancer's emotions are directed into his family life, Scorpio's emotions are directed into experiencing his inner personal power, and Pisces's emotions are directed into attaining a transcendent, spiritual consciousness.

——— AIR TRIPLICITY: GEMINI, LIBRA, AQUARIUS

Keywords for Mercury — planetary ruler of Gemini

> Conscious, analytical, rational mind
> Mental interests
> Mental learning processes
> Written and verbal communciation
> Friends
> Siblings

Keywords for Venus — planetary ruler of Libra

> Love, romance, marriage, partnership
> Beauty, harmony
> Art, music
> Money, financial security

Keywords for Uranus — planetary ruler of Aquarius

> Intuition
> Futurist vision, leading edge ideas
> Nonconformist, rebellious, revolutionary
> Mass communication, networking
> Science, high technology
> Spiritual awareness
> Planetary consciousness

Here also, the clues to the differences in the air triplicity are illuminated upon examining the planetary rulers' keywords. Just to take one example, all three air signs are concerned with communication, but their communication networks are different. Gemini is more interested in his personal friends, Libra is more interested in his romantic liasons, and Aquarius is involved in a large social and/or professional community network.

——————————— EARTH TRIPLICITY: TAURUS, VIRGO, CAPRICORN

Keywords for Venus — planetary ruler of Taurus

> Love, romance, marriage, partnership
> Beauty, harmony
> Art, music (In Taurus, this would be expressed through the earth element as crafts and country music, whereas in Libra it would be expressed as fine art.)
> Money, financial security

Keywords for Mercury — planetary ruler of Virgo

> Conscious, analytical, rational mind
> Mental interests
> Mental learning processes
> Written and verbal communication
> Friends
> Siblings

Keywords for Saturn – planetary ruler of Capricorn

> Life purpose, career
> Responsibility, karma
> Tests, limitations, delays, frustrations
> Focus

The three earth signs are grounded, common sense individuals but their areas of interests are different. The Venusian ruled Taurus is the sign well known for its pursuit of financial security. Mercurial Virgo is the curious, analytical earth sign who seeks provable and useable information. In contrast, the Saturnian influenced Capricorn is the career-oriented earth sign that is determined to fulfill his life purpose, despite all odds.

★ ▬▬▬▬▬▬▬▬▬▬ CHAPTER TEN

The Qualities From An Elemental Perspective

Like the four elements, the qualities express a basic underlying energy that shapes and forms each sign's initial character.

There are three qualities — cardinal, fixed and mutable — each of which express a different life approach. The cardinal quality is an active, fluctuating energy. In contrast, the fixed quality is a focused, concentrated energy recognized for its patience and stubbornness. The mutable quality is a reflective, mentally active and social energy.

▬▬ CLUES TO A QUALITY'S ELEMENTAL MAKEUP

Even though there is an unequal match between the *four* elements and the *three* qualities, I still feel that you can understand the qualities through an elemental framework.

It's easy to pick out the elemental associations of the cardinal and mutable qualities. The excitable, cardinal energy is obviously like the fire element. The four cardinal signs — Aries, Cancer, Libra and Capricorn — are the initiators of the zodiac always willing to try new activities. Aries seeks new physical experiences, Cancer seeks new emotional bonds, Libra seeks new romantic relationships and Capricorn seeks new career achievements.

The air element plays a large part in the intellectual, mutable signs — Gemini, Virgo, Sagittarius and Pisces. Like the air element, the mutable signs are always seeking to learn new information. Gemini seeks self awareness, Virgo seeks practical knowledge, Sagittarius thirsts for social and/or spiritual awareness and Pisces seeks to understand the mystical meaning behind life.

Also like the air element, the mutable signs seek to communicate their knowledge. Even the hermit-like Pisces is communicating in his solitude, although it may be with beings from other dimensions!

Now that we've analyzed the cardinal and mutable qualities, the questions remains about the fixed quality's elemental association. Is it water or is it earth — or both?

I think that a case can be made for both elements. Think for a second about the physical manifestations of the earth and water elements. Both earth and water (when it is frozen) can become solid, immovable masses. In a similar fashion, the fixed signs — Taurus, Leo, Scorpio, and Aquarius — are well known for their stubborn attitude which, if taken to an extreme, can result in a very rigid and closeminded personality.

The four fixed signs are very persistent, focused personalities. No matter what they're involved with, they're totally committed and unwilling to compromise their positions. For example, Taurus is well known for his stubbornness preserving his personal values, while Leo is famous for his insistence on individual creativity. Scorpio passionately pursues the depths of his inner personal power while socialized Aquarius holds fast to his social and/or spiritual visions.

Certainly the examples I've given above are just a few ways in which the qualities are expressed through each sign. Even so, it's easy to see how the qualities and the elements are interconnected. Before we leave this section, let's take one final look at the qualities from both the positive and the negative elemental characteristics. As you read through the list of traits think about their connection to the corresponding element.

Quality	Positive Traits	Negative Traits
1. Cardinal (Fire)	Stimulated	Overstimulated
	Energized	Scattered
	Active	Uncommitted
	Decisive	Reactive
	Openness	Uncontrollable
	Spontaneity	
2. Fixed (Earth & Water)	Persistent	Unyielding
	Determined	Obstinate
	Stubborn	Rigid
	Focused	Inflexible
	Concentrated	Afraid to change
	Controlled	
	Persevering	
	Committed	
	Steadfast	
	Loyal	
	Dedicated	
3. Mutable (Air)	Reflective	Indecisive
	Thoughtful	Mentally scattered
	Contemplative	Uncommitted
	Communicative	Uncertainty
	Understanding	Torn in two directions
	Detached	

QUALITY CLUES TO THE DIFFERENCES IN AN ELEMENTAL TRIPLICITY

As we saw earlier in this chapter, just because three signs share the same element does not mean that they are carbon copy duplicates. Just like planetary rulers, the qualities can be used to understand the differences that exist among the three signs in an elemental triplicity.

With every elemental triplicity the three qualities are equally represented. In other words, every triplicity has one cardinal sign, one fixed sign and one mutable sign (see below).

	Fire	Water	Air	Earth
Cardinal	Aries	Cancer	Libra	Capricorn
Fixed	Leo	Scorpio	Aquarius	Taurus
Mutable	Sagittarius	Pisces	Gemini	Virgo

Using the keywords in the previous chapter section you can begin to get additional insights into how the three signs in each triplicity express themselves differently.

FIRE SIGNS: ARIES (C), LEO (F), SAGITTARIUS (M)

Aries: Cardinal Fire

Out of all the fire signs, Aries is the most active. True to his stimulating, cardinal fire energy, he is the sensation junkie — always ready for a new experience. It's the excitement of a new challenge that energizes Aries, the daring and courageous adventurer. However, once the excitement dies down, the cardinal Aries is soon bored and leaves to seek yet another new experience.

With his positive cardinal fire energy, Aries is like a young child who eagerly tries new experiences. You never know what the Aries, with his wide-eyed childlike curiosity, will try next. Everything is stimulating to him if it's new.

Although the cardinal fire energy is great at initiating new ventures, it's weakness is that it lacks consistency and follow-through. Consequently, on the negative side, the cardinal fire energy creates a scattered Aries who jumps from one project to the next, never achieving his true potential.

Leo: Fixed Fire

A Leo can be as stubborn as a two year old throwing a temper tantrum. When he wants something, he is determined to get it no matter what.

"I am right and you are wrong," says the willful Leo who rigidly refuses to change his position. After all, that might mean changing his self awareness and that would be too threatening to the overly fixed Leo, who is stuck in his inauthentic, personality roles.

On a positive level, the fixed nature brings in a strong, confident and centered individual awareness. Committed and loyal to those he loves, his magnanimous nature is inspiring and uplifting.

Sagittarius: Mutable Fire

Mutable Sagittarius is the most reflective fire sign. As the eternal student of life, he constantly seeks new experiences and new information that will broaden his social and spiritual awareness.

If he integrates his information through a wholistic framework and transforms his knowledge into wisdom, he will become a wise philosopher and teacher. However, if he operates under the negative traits of the mutable energy, his unfocused mental curiosity will lead to many questions but few answers. This type of Sagittarius is like the college student who never graduates.

WATER SIGNS: CANCER (C), SCORPIO (F), PISCES (M)

Cancer: Cardinal Water

"I feel alive" and "I feel, therefore I am," are two sayings that illustrate the cardinal Cancer's life perspective. While the cardinal fire sign Aries feels alive through new physical experiences, the cardinal water sign Cancer feels alive through new emotional connections and expressions.

As the cardinal water sign of the zodiac, Cancer is the most emotionally volatile sign. His spontaneous, emotional reactions to situations can be overwhelming, not only to the Cancer but also to those around him.

On the other hand, his cardinal water is an emotional battery capable of recharging emotional well being. Like a mother, Cancer is the emotional nurturer that makes us all feel good again.

Scorpio: Fixed Water

No sign is more emotionally fixed than the water sign Scorpio. Like an ice cube that is frozen (fixed) water, the Scorpio controls and contains his emotions. Keeping his innermost feelings from public view, he is mistakenly accused of being a cold and unfeeling person. Nothing could be further from the truth. All too often people will say to the Scorpio, "Stop being so intense!" or "Lighten up!" Unfortunately, such comments only irritate the Scorpio.

"Don't they understand I'm a fixed water sign? Ice doesn't melt instantly, you know," says the exasperated Scorpio.

Also like an ice cube, the Scorpio *freezes* his emotional memories. Holding on tight to his past emotional experiences, the fixed Scorpio remembers everything. When the memories are positive, the Scorpio will use them as a motivational springboard. However, when the memories are of past emotional traumas, the Scorpio will find himself trapped in a corner by his past emotional reactions. The only way out of this predicament is to forgive and move on, but this is a very difficult task for the obstinate, fixed Scorpio.

Pisces: Mutable Water

Whether it be through psychology, religion or transcendent altered states of consciousness, mutable Pisces reflects upon the human condition. Understanding the emotional joys and sorrows in his life and others, Pisces's intellectual disassociation is transformed into compassionate concern and caring.

More than any other sign, he is the "social worker/confessional priest." Sensing his compassion, people flock to the Pisces to tell their tales of woe and to receive sympathy and solace.

Although the Pisces appears to be the saint of the zodiac, sometimes he is nothing more than a doormat who can't say no. Unable to confront those individuals who are wasting his time and not using his advice, the indecisive Pisces gives them one more chance — over and over again. Until he learns to say no he'll be emotionally scattered between all his rescue operations.

—————————— AIR SIGNS: GEMINI(M), LIBRA (C), AQUARIUS (F)

Gemini: Mutable Air

Gemini is the mutable air sign and since the mutable quality has an air-like energy, it's as if Gemini has a double air energy. Torn between two opposing points of view, the Gemini is often uncommitted and indecisive in thought and in action.

"Every point of view has a pro and a con," explains the dualistic Gemini who can't firmly commit himself one way or another.

On the negative level, mutable Gemini is the chatterbox airhead of the zodiac who superficially talks about everything to anyone. He always knows a little about a lot but his blustery air pretends to know much more. His pursuit of trivial knowledge may get him a spot on a game show, but it won't help him improve his life.

In contrast, the positive mutable Gemini is a rational, objective thinker who likes to research a problem and know all the facts before he makes a decision. Disassociating himself from personal emotional biases, he can clearly perceive the truth in a situation. With clarity of mind and eloquence in word, he makes an excellent communicator.

Libra: Cardinal Air

Whether attending a party or planning one, the Libra is an active social individual who is always willing to meet new people. Stimulated by social interactions, the Libra comes alive amidst a social gathering.

Ruled by Venus, the planet of love, the uncommitted Libra is geared towards finding a romantic liason. In particular, his cardinal energy is enthralled by the beginning romantic excitement that a new love interest brings. Once committed, the Libra expends a lot of energy to keep the romance in his relationship alive (candlelit dinners, Valentine's Day presents etc.).

Hating to be alone, the overstimulated cardinal Libra will purposely overbook his social calendar. If he's already in a relationship, the Libra will spend too much time on relationship concerns. Single or married, the overextended Libra loses his individuality to a social identity.

Aquarius: Fixed Air

With the positive power of the fixed quality, the Aquarius has the ability to discipline his mind and concentrate on the task at hand. When he finally finishes his deliberations and reaches a decision, he is very committed. However, if he is working under the negative aspects of the fixed quality, his loyalty to a particular idea often stems from a fear of change. This type of Aquarius has a rigid, closed and inflexible mental attitude that absolutely refuses to consider new possibilities.

The fixed quality is a powerful energy. As the fixed air sign, Aquarius understands that ideas have the power to mobilize people and to initiate social change. Combining his natural networking ability with desire to actualize his ideas, he's the perfect lobbyist or politician. Like a presidential candidate who campaigns for years, the Aquarius has the perseverance and the mental stamina to communicate his message over and over again.

Ronald Reagan is a good example of a fixed Aquarius native. Famous for his communication skills and dedicated to his political ideas, he initiated a new political era. Depending on your political stance, you may perceive him as a positive Aquarius who brought important new ideas or a negative Aquarius whose inflexibility created economic and social problems. No matter how you look at it, true to his fixed Aquarius nature, he persevered for two terms and changed America's direction.

—————— EARTH SIGNS: TAURUS (F), VIRGO (M), CAPRICORN (C)

Taurus: Fixed Earth

All the fixed signs have tremendous power. Leo has personality power, Scorpio has emotional/psychic power, Aquarius has mental power and Taurus, the fixed earth sign, has material power. Born with a practical understanding of economics and an appreciation for the finer things in life, the Taurus perseveres to create a materially comfortable and financially secure life. (Isn't it interesting that a profitable stock market climate is called a bull market?)

Now there's nothing wrong in enjoying material pleasure and certainly Taurus's keen business sense should be applauded. However, for the overly fixed Taurus who is rooted in earthly desire, life becomes nothing more than a greedy accumulation of property and a fixation on his bank balance and stock portfolio status.

Not every Taurus is this fixed — but every Taurus rightly deserves the adjective bullheaded. Not one to change his mind easily, the Taurus takes one thing at a time and slowly (but surely) works it through. The slow moving Taurus isn't dumb, but he is very thorough and conservative. If you're trying to change his mind, offer practical solutions and then be patient. Like a bull, the Taurus hates to be agitated.

Virgo: Mutable Earth

The office manager of the zodiac, mutable Virgo is always busy **thinking** about appointments, schedules, projects — you name it and he has it on his list. Like the worker bee, the Virgo is a tireless worker who finds it hard to relax. There's always another chore or errand that has to be done.

An organizer par excellence, the Virgo's mental, mutable energy stimulates his work productivity. Thoughtful and reflective about his responsibilities, his work displays the attention he pays to details that others would have easily forgotten.

On the surface, it may seem that the overburdened Virgo hates his work. In actuality, he likes to be organized and without his daily work routines, the Virgo would feel empty and confused.

However, when the overextended, mutable Virgo is torn between a multitude of uncompleted projects and pressing deadlines, he's a frazzled worrywart. Relax, Virgo, the world won't fall apart if you take a day off from thinking about your duties. Your mental and physical health are more important than completing your scheduled deadlines.

Capricorn: Cardinal Earth

Combine the active cardinal quality with the stable earth element and you get an energized worker who's thrilled by new business opportunities and new business contacts. Life revolves around the Capricorn's business deals, especially the successful ones and the new ones that are brewing.

Talk to my cousin, Lynn Crisler Wilford, and you'll get a good idea how the cardinal quality propels the earth sign Capricorn. As a media consultant, she's always on the go, travelling from one television station to the next. Whether you call her at 8am or at 8pm, she's probably on the phone or in conference, still conducting business.

Don't feel sorry for her though, her cardinal earth energy loves the challenge.

A Capricorn who is under the negative aspect of the cardinal quality is a workaholic scattered between too many business commitments. Placing too much emphasis on their career, the Capricorn will keep working long hours even when the challenge and the joy of working is long gone. Trying desperately to regain the thrill that work used to bring, he uncontrollably works himself into the ground.

★ ▬▬▬ PART FOUR

THE SECONDARY ELEMENTS—
MY ORIGINAL THEORY

▬▬▬▬▬▬▬ CHAPTER ELEVEN
The Theory Of Secondary Elements

▬▬▬▬▬▬▬ CHAPTER TWELVE
Identifying The Secondary Elements

★ ▬▬▬▬▬▬▬▬▬▬▬ **CHAPTER ELEVEN**

The Theory Of Secondary Elements

I believe that each sign has a secondary element that strongly influences, but never overwhelms, the sign's primary elemental nature. This is my original theory which I developed around 1974-1975.

At first this may seem like a radical departure from traditional astrological thought. However, as I will show in the next chapter, the existence of a secondary elemental system has always been present, although until now, never before clearly delineated.

As with the ruling planets and the qualities, the secondary elements point out the differences between the signs in an elemental triplicity. In addition, they also show similarities between those signs that share the same secondary element.

The secondary elemental system provides a fresh, new way of examining the signs and understanding their motivations. Using the secondary elemental system may give you new insights and integrate your astrological knowledge. That's what it has done for me and my students.

However, instead of taking my word, challenge yourself first. All the clues to a sign's secondary element are contained in the previous chapters. If you'd like, review the information you've already learned (Exercise #1) and then try to figure out each sign's secondary element (Exercise #2).

_____ EXERCISE #1: ZODIAC REVIEW

Use this exercise to review the signs and to write down any important impressions or keywords.

Fire Signs: Aries, Leo, Sagittarius

Aries:
Ruling Planet: _____
Quality:_____
Keywords: _____
_____
_____

Leo:
Ruling Planet: _____
Quality:_____
Keywords: _____
_____
_____

Sagittarius:
Ruling Planet: _____
Quality:_____
Keywords: _____
_____
_____

Water Signs: Cancer, Scorpio, Pisces

Cancer:
Ruling Planet: _____
Quality:_____
Keywords: _____
_____
_____

Scorpio:
Ruling Planet: ——————————————————————
Quality:——————————————————————————————
Keywords: ————————————————————————————
——————————————————————————————————————
——————————————————————————————————————

Pisces:
Ruling Planet: ——————————————————————
Quality:——————————————————————————————
Keywords: ————————————————————————————
——————————————————————————————————————
——————————————————————————————————————

Air Signs: Gemini, Libra, Aquarius

Gemini:
Ruling Planet: ——————————————————————
Quality:——————————————————————————————
Keywords: ————————————————————————————
——————————————————————————————————————
——————————————————————————————————————

Libra:
Ruling Planet: ——————————————————————
Quality:——————————————————————————————
Keywords: ————————————————————————————
——————————————————————————————————————
——————————————————————————————————————

Aquarius:
Ruling Planet: ——————————————————————
Quality:——————————————————————————————
Keywords: ————————————————————————————
——————————————————————————————————————
——————————————————————————————————————

Earth Signs: Taurus, Virgo, Capricorn

Taurus:
Ruling Planet: _____
Quality:_____
Keywords: _____
_____
_____

Virgo:
Ruling Planet: _____
Quality:_____
Keywords: _____
_____
_____

Capricorn:
Ruling Planet: _____
Quality:_____
Keywords: _____
_____
_____

_____ EXERCISE #2: DISCOVERING THE SECONDARY ELEMENTS

Before you begin, here are a few points to keep in mind:

1. The secondary element is never the same as the primary element. In other words, a fire sign cannot have a modifying secondary fire element.

2. Within an elemental triplicity, each sign has a different secondary element. For example, in the air triplicity of Gemini, Libra and Aquarius, one air sign is modified by earth, another air sign is modified by fire and the third air sign is modified by water.

3. The secondary elements are equally distributed. Three signs always share a common secondary element.

Whether you're a beginning or an advanced astrology student, give yourself the opportunity to discover the secondary elements. It's a chance for you to integrate your astrological knowledge.

Fire Signs: Aries, Leo, Sagittarius

Aries: Fire/_____

Primary Element: Fire
Secondary Element: _____
Reasons Why: _____
_____
_____
_____

Leo: Fire/_____

Primary Element: Fire
Secondary Element: _____
Reasons Why: _____

_____

_____

_____

Sagittarius: Fire/_____

Primary Element: Fire
Secondary Element: _____
Reasons Why: _____

_____

_____

_____

Water Signs: Cancer, Scorpio, Pisces

Cancer: Water/_____

Primary Element: Water
Secondary Element: _____
Reasons Why: _____

_____

_____

_____

Scorpio: Water/_____

Primary Element: Water
Secondary Element: _____
Reasons Why: _____

_____

_____

_____

Pisces: Water/_____

Primary Element: Water
Secondary Element: _____
Reasons Why: _____
_____
_____
_____

Air Signs: Gemini, Libra, Aquarius

Gemini: Air/_____

Primary Element: Air
Secondary Element: _____
Reasons Why: _____
_____
_____
_____

Libra: Air/_____

Primary Element: Air
Secondary Element: _____
Reasons Why: _____
_____
_____
_____

Aquarius: Air/_____

Primary Element: Air
Secondary Element: _____
Reasons Why: _____
_____
_____
_____

Earth Signs: Taurus, Virgo, Capricorn

Taurus: Earth/_____

Primary Element: Earth
Secondary Element: _____
Reasons Why: _____

_____

_____

_____

Virgo: Earth/_____

Primary Element: Earth
Secondary Element: _____
Reasons Why: _____

_____

_____

_____

Capricorn: Earth/_____

Primary Element: Earth
Secondary Element: _____
Reasons Why: _____

_____

_____

_____

★ ■■■■■■■■■■■■■■■ **CHAPTER TWELVE**

Identifying The Secondary Elements

Congratulations to those readers who challenged themselves to discover the secondary elements! Now, here's my theory.

■■■■■■■■■■■■■■■■■■■■■■■■■ **THE FIRE SIGNS**

ARIES: FIRE/EARTH

Primary Element: Fire
Secondary Element: Earth

Don't worry if you struggled over this sign's secondary element. I did, too.

When I initially started putting together my secondary element theory, I strongly considered the possibility that there might be pure signs that weren't modified by a secondary element.

For quite a long time I thought Aries might be a pure fire sign. After all, it's the first fire sign, a cardinal sign and ruled by the fiery planet Mars. Aries natives are like flickering flames — always on the go, they can't stay still. How could it be anything but pure fire?

Initially it sounds plausible, but the question remains, "Why should there be an exception?" After all, the zodiac's elemental framework is a consistent one with the four elements equally divided among the twelve signs.

Logic dictates that Aries, like every other sign, has a secondary element. I was convinced of my secondary element choices for Leo and Sagittarius. Consequently, the process of elimination left the earth element as Aries's secondary element. Here too, I struggled because my perceptions of Aries at the time did not include a strong earth element influence.

Looking at earth's keywords, I couldn't understand how a secondary earth element could possibly fit. "A secondary earth element would calm down, perhaps even inhibit, the Aries's excitable, spontaneous fire energy," I argued with myself.

The breakthrough for me came when I finally put into perspective the importance of Aries's position as the zodiac's first sign. It is here in the beginning sign Aries that consciousness in the physical world is born and exists in a primitive and primordial state. This primeval awareness is the key to understanding Aries's fire/earth character.

Within this context, the earth element represents the beginning of a physical consciousness. The Aries's primary fire element is grounded by its secondary earth element, but not in a conscious, organized fashion. Instead, the earth element's natural inclination for order is expressed through nature's fundamental, biological systems.

With such a strong, primitive physical awareness, Aries, more than any other sign, experiences life like a wild animal and quite appropriately, the wild ram is Aries's symbol. In touch with the essence of life's physical currents, Aries's life order is instinctive and biological.

The fire element by itself indicates consciousness, but it is the secondary earth element that brings the Aries fire into the physical realm. No wonder then that Aries is a physical sensation junkie who revels in experiencing new and different physical sensations.

The secondary earth element also helps to explain the Mars's rulership of Aries. Mars is the planet associated with physical vitality and sex, a basic, biological drive. It's not coincidence that this sign exudes a raw, sexual, physical magnetism and enjoys in particular, sexual physical release.

As the wild ram, Aries is determined to keep his freedom and independent nature. Influenced by his primordial secondary earth element, he lives according to nature's laws, not society's laws. Like a wild animal, Aries is concerned with survival, but survival in these modern times is a battle to maintain his primitive spirit in the face of an ever increasing computerized and technocratic society.

LEO: FIRE/WATER

Primary Element: Fire
Secondary Element: Water

Every actor must be able to fully reach into his imagination and his emotional depths in order to create a new role and captivate the audience. In effect, how well an actor can summon up the water element will determine his acting ability.

Leo is famous as the resident zodiacal actor, but it's not his fire energy alone that gives him such theatrical flair. Imbued with the emotional creative energy of the secondary water element, his dramatic acting ability comes from his fire/water mixture.

Due to his secondary water element, one of Leo's powers is the ability to create an image (a water keyword). This image creating ability is expressed through its zodiacal connection with the lion whose reputation as the powerful "King of the Jungle" is all show.

A second power, which can also be understood through the Leo's fire/water elemental makeup, is his ability to charismatically stimulate and enhance an audience's emotions. With his secondary water influence, the Leo understands emotional motivations. Combining this emotional sensitivity with his fiery energy, he is the charismatic leader who inspires our dreams and emotional hopes.

Used in a positive way, the Leo's fire/water nature is creative, passionate, and sensitive. However, when negative secondary water traits such as emotional insecurity or moodiness are activated, the Leo hides behind a contrived role. Too scared to express his individuality, he acts in order to hide his feelings and/or to gain emotional approval. No longer the shining star that illuminates the spirit within, this is the Leo whose image, like the lion's, is false. As a fixed sign, the danger exists that he may become emotionally stuck in his inauthentic self expression. (Remember, the fixed quality can have a water energy. Leo's fixed quality is one of the clues to its strong emotional nature.)

SAGITTARIUS: FIRE/AIR

Primary Element: Fire
Secondary Element: Air

It's not enough for the fiery Sagittarius to experience life, with his secondary air element he wants to learn about and understand life. Consequently, the Sagittarius is the eternal student in search of meaningful, new information that expands his awareness and integrates his life experiences.

There are many clues that suggest Sagittarius's air nature. First of all, it's a mutable sign and like the air element, the mutable quality is mentally oriented.

A second clue to Sagittarius's fire/air energy is Jupiter, its ruling planet. Associated with higher knowledge, education, philosophy and culture, Jupiter is an intellectual, philosophically reflective planet. Fueled by Jupiter's strong mental curiosity, the Sagittarius's daily mantra is "Why? Why? Why?"

The third most visual clue to Sagittarius's fire/air makeup is its mythological symbol, the centaur. The centaur is a creature who is half horse (lower torso and legs) and half human (upper torso and head). The horse half symbolizes Sagittarius's impatient, unrestrained fire energy, while the human half portrays the Sagittarius's mental inquisitiveness.

Legends about the centaurs illustrate their fire/air combination. On one hand there are tales that, depicting the centaurs as a wild and lawless race, show their fiery, aggressive nature. On the other hand, there are stories about a few exceptionally wise centaurs who were highly respected. One such centaur was Chiron. According to legend, Chiron was instructed by the gods Apollo and Artemis and later taught such notables as Hercules, Asclepius, Achilles and the argonaut

Jason. Like the centaur Chiron, Sagittarius is a skilled teacher who loves to communicate his knowledge and share his life experiences. Wise like Chiron, the positive Sagittarius leader rules with his wisdom and ethics. (Where Aries is a leader through his actions and Leo is a leader through his charisma and image.)

In addition to his ongoing educational pursuits, the Sagittarius's strong communication skills and socialized awareness also point to a secondary air element. Here again, his mutable quality and Jupiter rulership help us to understand this fire sign's need for social interaction. Combining the communicative mutable energy with Jupiter's enthusiastic social energy, it's easy to see why Sagittarius is the most socially active and talkative fire sign. Always reaching out to meet new people and make new friends, the sociable Sagittarius communicates like an air sign. Even though he's not an air sign, he rivals Gemini for the title chatterbox of the zodiac.

In conclusion, when the negative aspects of the air element are operating, the Sagittarius is a hyperactive student who accumulates more information than he can possibly digest. Jumping from one subject to the next, the mentally scattered Sagittarius's quest for knowledge turns into trivial pursuit.

THE WATER SIGNS

CANCER: WATER/EARTH

Primary Element: Water
Secondary Element: Earth

Ruled by the moon and symbolized by the crab, Cancer's water element is obvious. However, if you look just a little further, you'll find that the moon and the crab contain clues indicating earth's secondary elemental status.

It's a well known fact that the moon influences life's biological rhythms. This connection to nature suggests an underlying earth element energy.

The crab's protective shell also suggests the earth element's presence. In addition, by dwelling in the water and on the land, the crab's habitat illustrates his water/earth nature.

With his emotional water influenced by earth, the Cancer seeks emotional stability and security. It's not enough for the Cancer to feel an emotional rapport; he wants to ground this feeling and create a tangible, emotional bond. No wonder that the Cancer is so family oriented. For good or for bad, the family unit is a permanent (earth keyword) emotional connection.

The Cancer appreciates the importance of tradition and the part it plays in affirming and establishing emotional continuity. Whether it's Christmas, holidays, golden anniversaries or family reunions, the water/earth Cancer cherishes the events that bind us together.

When a Cancer is emotionally involved with someone, his water/earth character wants to provide for their every need on both emotional and physical levels. For example, if you're sick, the Cancer will offer you emotional support (water) and chicken soup (earth). No matter how low you may feel, they'll coach you back to emotional and physical health.

A Cancer's support feels great when it is freely given but feels overwhelmingly suffocating when it's part of a ploy to maintain and control a relationship. When the negative traits of the secondary earth element are in effect, the Cancer's inner stability (positive water/earth) is lost and he seeks personal emotional security and self worth through another person (negative water/earth). Then when this relationship fails, he is devastated and feels lost. Cancer, always remember that your home is inside, not outside.

SCORPIO: WATER/FIRE

Primary Element: Water
Secondary Element: Fire

Visualize an active volcano located deep below the ocean's surface. Now imagine that the volcano erupts and its hot lava rapidly heats the ocean water. As you imagine the water's rising temperatures, let yourself also feel its fiery boil.

This image of the underwater volcano best describes the Scorpio's water/fire character. With an active volcano lurking underneath his cool exterior, it's easy to understand why the Scorpio is famous for his passionate and forceful desire. Influencing the Scorpio's watery emotions, the fire's heated desire creates high pitched emotional intensity.

Consequently, it's easy to understand why the fiery planet Mars was Scorpio's original ruling planet. Mars is the planet associated with personal power and sex; Scorpio is famous for his sexually aware and power-oriented nature. However, unlike Aries who is still ruled by Mars, it's not physical power or physical sexual release that the water Scorpio desires. Instead, he seeks emotional and psychic power and in sex, he welcomes the opportunity to explore his hidden emotional desires and his psychic abilities.

Concerned with the transformational abilities of his inner consciousness, many Scorpios find themselves deeply involved in studying psychology, astrology and psychic subjects. Ruled by Pluto, the planet associated with the mythological god of the hidden underworld, and spurred on by his water/fire nature to illuminate the unknown, the Scorpio is driven to uncover life's hidden mysteries and powers.

Learning how to wisely use his power is an important Scorpio lesson. If he works from the negative side of his secondary fire element, he is an emotionally charged, reactive individual bent on revenge, who strikes out at others with his poisonous scorpion stinger. Whether through hurtful words and actions, or through harmful psychic vibrations, the emotionally aroused water/fire Scorpio covertly fights back.

However, if the Scorpio uses the positive energy of his secondary fire element, then the inner fire purifies his emotional waters and transforms his consciousness. Like the mythological phoenix who dies in flames only to be reborn in his ashes, the Scorpio is emotionally reborn in the wake of his emotional endings.

"All endings bring new beginning," says the Plutonian Scorpio who appreciates life and death's intricate duet.

PISCES: WATER/AIR

Primary Element: Water
Secondary Element: Air

Unlike Cancer who is grounded by his secondary earth element and Scorpio, who is stabilized by his fixed quality, the mutable Pisces is the most sensitive and fragile water sign. In part this fragility comes from its dissipative secondary air element which widely disperses the Pisces's primary water element. Imagine a mist or a fog and you'll get a good idea of the Pisces's water/air makeup.

There are a number of clues that indicate a strong air element presence. First, Pisces is a mutable sign and the mutable quality has an air energy. Second, its symbol of a pair of fish points to a *dual* nature (air keyword), as does its glyph. Third, from a mythological perspective, the god Neptune rules the seas and oceans. The vastness of Neptune's watery domain indicates an expansive water influence, once again suggesting a water/air combination.

With the curiosity and the discriminating eye of the air element, the Pisces looks into the watery inner levels of life and sees our deep unconscious motivations. Although this is a talent that can be used for tremendous good, it also poses a serious dilemma. Seeing inner realities that others are oblivious to, his insights are often invalidated, even though they are accurate.

Living as a sensitive in the physical world is not an easy task and Pisces welcomes a break from the ignorant and limited world that most people call home. Consequently, Pisces loves to disassociate (air keyword) from normal reality and instead enter the astral, inner space dimensions.

Depending on the Pisces's level of consciousness, he will disassociate in a number of different ways. The spiritually conscious Pisces may tap into his inner consciousness through out-of-body experiences, trance channelling, meditation or prayer (just to name a few possibilities). I have a good Pisces friend who disassociates her spirit from the body to such a degree that she actually transports herself to another dimension. When she wants to take a break from the physical world, she goes to a beach and relaxes. It's not a fantasy; it's a consciousness teleportation. When she is gone on an excursion, people notice that her eyes are vacant, just as if her spirit is totally gone from her body — which it has!

With mental air also stirring up his vivid imagination, the Pisces can easily create any fantasy scenario. Activating his right brain potential, the imaginative Pisces disassociates and goes into an all-absorbing, creative, trance state.

So far we've seen the air element's positive influence. However, if the secondary air element is operating on a negative level, the Pisces is a weak-willed, indecisive and ambivalent person. At worst, he is a very evasive and deceitful individual who thinks nothing about making up untrue stories and lying to himself and others. With such a vivid imagination, he may actually believe in his stories to such an extent that others are equally convinced they are true. Out of touch and out of control, this Pisces often uses drugs and alcohol to escape into his fantasy world and dream away his life's problems.

_____**THE AIR SIGNS**

GEMINI: AIR/FIRE

Primary Element: Air
Secondary Element: Fire

"Can we talk?" should be the Gemini's trademark. Stimulated by his secondary fire element, this mutable air sign loves the opportunity to exchange ideas and gather new information. Whether he's participating in a talk show, meeting new people or talking to new friends, the Gemini comes alive when he communicates. No wonder so many people know the Gemini.

Inflamed by his secondary fire element, he loves a heated discussion and will purposely play devil's advocate just to make the discussions more exciting. With a good supply of hot air (air/fire), he's a good debator, but watch out for an argument if the fire gets too hot.

Thanks to his spirited secondary fire element, Gemini can be a dynamic speaker and a convincing salesperson. However, if the fire element is scattered and unfocused, this creates a nervous, airhead, chatterbox who flits from topic to topic, not noticing or caring if anyone is listening.

Curious as a cat and energized by his passionate secondary fire element, the Gemini aggressively seeks new information through classes, books and conversations. His active mind learns quickly, but with a short attention span, he's easily bored. Capable of learning many different things at once, his spice of life is intellectual variety. However, if he overextends himself (negative air/fire), then the quality of his information will be shallow and superficial. This type of Gemini makes a better game show contestant than an intellectual scholar.

LIBRA: AIR/EARTH

Primary Element: Air
Secondary Element: Earth

Thanks to his secondary earth element, Libra is the most conventional and traditional air sign. Unlike air/fire Gemini who enjoys a rapid succession of acquaintances, the air/earth Libra seeks a reliable and dependable social network. Taking the advice of his serious secondary earth element, Libra takes his relationships very seriously.

Like Gemini and Aquarius, the Libra enjoys socializing and meeting new people, although he is the most reserved air sign. Influenced by the cautious and hesitant earth element, his social interactions are polite and well mannered. Understanding the role of etiquette and knowing how to use it, this natural born diplomat can turn an awkward first meeting into a pleasant and cordial encounter. In part his diplomatic success stems from his airy Venusian grace, but it also stems from his ability to remember and utilize traditional social courtesies.

Above all, he is the judicious air sign who knows that every story has two sides that should be equally examined. Where the air/fire Gemini speaks without thinking of the consequences, the air/earth Libra patiently withholds judgment while considering the facts. Like a judge hearing a case, he weighs the scales of justice (his symbol), and then delivers his opinion.

The scales of justice are famous as Libra's symbol and glyph, and rightly so, since Libra spends his life seeking balance, harmony, and order. This drive for harmonious order, which is symbolically expressed through the scales and its Venusian rulership, are the biggest clues that indicate earth is Libra's secondary element.

However, if he is persuaded by the negative aspects of the secondary earth element, then his drive for harmony becomes a drive for security. Unable to confront his inner instability, he holds on tight to a harmonious external facade that belies his inner, disharmonious feelings. Staying in a relationship for security and social status, he is imprisoned by his narrow, negative, secondary element earth.

Libra has to learn that harmony is an inner state of mind (positive air/earth), not an outer condition that can be permanently secured (negative air/earth).

AQUARIUS: AIR/WATER

Primary Element: Air
Secondary Element: Water

Did you ever mistakenly think that Aquarius was a water sign? It's a common mistake since the water bearer is Aquarius's symbol and its glyph looks like ocean waves. In addition, it's a fixed sign and as I mentioned in Chapter Ten, the fixed quality can have a water energy.

Influenced by his secondary water element, Aquarius is the compassionate air sign who roots for the underdog and who helps society's less fortunate individuals.

My sister, Carrie, is a good example of an Aquarius whose professional work shows her caring nature. In her first job as a nurse practitioner, she counseled drug dependent veterans. Her next job was helping the homeless. I always wonder who my reform-minded, Aquarian sister will help next.

An Aquarius loves to be part of a extended social network and many times they can be found in the forefront of new social movements. In large part this is due to Uranus, its unconventional, intuitive and futuristic ruling planet. However, it's also because of his psychic secondary water element that the Aquarius is able to perceive, through his sixth sense, future social trends and issues.

Water is the element associated with psychic awareness and the unconscious mind. With the power of water's unconscious forces influencing his intellectual consciousness, the Aquarius is naturally curious about inner mental powers. This curiosity will lead him into alternative, nontraditional studies, so don't be surprised if you meet a lot of Aquarians in astrological and New Age circles!

Whatever movement the Aquarius chooses to be part of, one thing is for certain — once the fixed Aquarius has chosen a particular cause, he is intellectually and emotionally committed. However, as the air/water sign, Aquarius is more idealistic than realistic. Watch out, Aquarius, for allowing your watery nature to flood your mind with too much emotional idealism. No, you can't save the whole world, but yes, you can make a difference.

THE EARTH SIGNS

TAURUS: EARTH/WATER

Primary Element: Earth
Secondary Element: Water

Mother Nature resides in the garden tended by the earth nurturing Taurus native. With a green thumb that can make any flower bloom bright, the Taurus has a special emotional bond with the nature kingdom. It's not only his basic gardening skill that works miracles, it's his inner feelings and loving attention that makes the difference.

This inner connection with the physical realm is a big indication that water is Taurus's secondary element. A strong visual clue lies in its glyph which can be seen as a crescent moon lying on top of planet earth.   Mythological legends also support Taurus's watery background energy. Aphrodite, the Greek equivalent of the Roman goddess Venus, was born in water. The fertility goddess Maia, who was honored by the Romans on May Day, was a sea nymph. Even the Hyades, a group of stars that form the face of the bull in the Taurus constellation, were associated with nourishing spring rains.

With the emotional water element influencing his primary earth element, the Taurus knows that the key to a good life lies in material (earth) and emotional (water) well being. No wonder that Taurus is the earth sign that wants to feel good.

Once you understand his secondary water influence, it's easy to understand how the common sense, practical Taurus can also be so moved by the first daffodil of spring or a beautiful sunset.

However, as important as a nature retreat is to the Taurus's spirit, so too is an emotional, loving relationship. Ruled by Venus, the planet of personal life, the Taurus yearns for a fulfilling physical and emotional relationship. When a relationship is absent in his life, the earth/water Taurus feels an inner emptiness. Often he tries to fill this void with various material possessions. Try as he may, though, material substitutes are not as fulfilling as a loving relationship.

VIRGO: EARTH/AIR

Primary Element: Earth
Secondary Element: Air

With a mutable quality and the ruling planet Mercury, it's obvious that the Virgo's primary earth element is influenced by a secondary air element. As the planet that co-rules Virgo and Gemini (the air/fire sign), Mercury is the "thinking planet," associated with the conscious, logical, mental processes. Sharing the same ruling planet, Gemini and Virgo both have strong mental natures. Because of their different primary elements, the two signs do not think alike. Airy Gemini loves to speculate on theories and learn new facts without necessarily considering their usefulness. In contrast, the earthy Virgo only wants practical, reliable (earth keywords) knowledge.

With an eye for detail and a desire to know every single pertinent fact, no matter how small, the Virgo patiently (earth influence) acquires specialized knowledge (air influence). This aspect of Virgo is represented by the Roman goddess Minerva (Athene is the Greek goddess equivalent), whose birth from Jupiter's (Zeus) head indicates a dominant mental nature. Modelling himself after Minerva, the goddess of wisdom who is famous for her extremely technical, skilled information, the Virgo is driven to attain a high level of expertise on whatever subject peaks his curiosity. By the way, one subject that usually intrigues the Virgo is the field of health and in particular, the connection between physical health (earth) and mental health (air).

One thing a Virgo has to watch out for is going overboard in tracking down each and every detail. When the inquisitive secondary air element becomes overly stimulated, the Virgo loses himself in a whirlwind of details that cloud his investigation's main purpose. It's as if he's lost on uncharted mental back roads and can't find his way back to the main highway.

Likewise, the Virgo has to be careful about overanalyzing each and every situation. Granted, he has the gift to see details that others miss. However, when his active, analytical mind combines with his earth's drive for order in a negative way, the Virgo is an overly critical, regimented person who can't relax unless everything is in perfect order. Needless to say, this can drive people crazy, which is not Virgo's intention. Influenced by the social air element, this responsible earth sign reaches out to help people with his time and his well earned knowledge. In his mind, he's just trying to perfect an imperfect world.

CAPRICORN: EARTH/FIRE

Primary Element: Earth
Secondary Element: Fire

Despite a common impression that Capricorn is cold, reserved and aloof, the Capricorn is actually an earthy individual with a strong fiery undercurrent. However, like the water/fire Scorpio whose secondary fire element is hidden from sight, the earth/fire Capricorn often contains his fiery drives below a conventional, traditional, outer personality. Whereas the Scorpio's image is an underwater volcano (fire in water), the Capricorn brings to mind our planet earth, whose outer crust conceals an extremely active, hot, molten core (fire in earth).

Besides the cardinal energy which points to the possibility of a secondary fire element, there are also a number of mythological clues. Remembering the fire element is associated with passion and sexual energy, it's interesting to note that Pan, a goat-like mythological Greek god, was famous for his sexual lust. Also similar to Pan in both appearance and sexual appetite were the satyrs, woodland divinities with small horns on their head, pointed ears and cloven hoofs.

Whether in his personal life or his professional life, nothing but nothing, can stop this ambitious, cardinal sign. While Capricorn's primary earth nature accounts for his patient, productive character, it does not account for his highly competitive nature, his drive to succeed and his desire to make a name for himself. This unrelenting, passionate drive for power and success comes from his ambitious secondary fire elemental influence. (Note all the fire keywords I've used in this paragraph to describe the Capricorn's personality.)

On a negative level, the Capricorn is a power hungry, ruthless individual who uses people to reach the top. With a survival of the fittest attitude (reminiscent of fiery Aries), the Capricorn wants to win, no matter what the cost. Not caring who gets hurt, he believes that the end (winning) justifies the means.

On a positive level, his secondary fire element challenges his primary earth nature to constantly move forward, to assume greater responsibilities, create new goals and in the process, actualize his true potential.

In the end, the Capricorn is the opportunist who patiently waits for his chance while others impatiently give up on their goals and change their dreams. When opportunity knocks, the Capricorn is ready to spring into action, but even when success arrives, the Capricorn can't stand still. Achievement is in his blood and the Capricorn is forever striving to reach new heights.

★ ▬▬▬▬▬▬▬▬▬▬▬ **CONCLUSION**

Now that you have an in-depth approach to the elements of astrology, it's time to challenge yourself and increase your astrological fluency.

As I have presented, there are many ways to learn astrology. Whether you use all of my suggestions or only a few, if you listen to your intuition, you will find the answers you seek.

Always remember that your astrological ability depends on two things:

1. **your commitment to learning the astrological language**
2. **your personal power**

I wish you much success in your astrological journey.

★ ■■■■■■■■■■■■■■■■■■■■■■■■■■■■■■■ **APPENDIX**

Additional Answers To Chapter Eight Exercises

There are many different answers for the exercises in Chapter Eight. The following answers are just a few possibilities.

THE ELEMENTS' PHYSICAL FORMS

FIRE: The sun, lava, a forest fire, fireworks, bonfire, flame on a gas burner, flame on a matchstick, lit birthday candles

WATER: A flood, an underground stream, a lake or pond, a waterfall, an ocean wave, tap water, a glass of water, a raindrop, liquids, an ice cube, hail

AIR: The jetstream, a tornado, a typhoon, a hurricane, a squall, a sea breeze, a guest of wind, a draft, a cough, a sneeze

EARTH: Forests, boulders, rocks, gravel, mud, sand, gems, nature (all living plants)

PHYSICAL INTERACTIONS

1. How is Fire Affected By:

a. Water?
Scenario: Firemen hose down a raging fire.
Result: Eventually, the water douses the fire.

b. Air?
Scenario #1: A camper fans the flames of a small fire.
Result: The additional air fuels the fire's flames and the small fire burns more wood.
Scenario #2: The little girl blows out her birthday cake candles.
Result: A strong breath of air blows out the candle flames.

c. Earth?
Scenario: A campfire is smothered by a bucket of dirt.
Result: The dirt destroys fire.

2. How Is Water Affected By:

a. Fire?
Scenario: A pot of water is placed on a lit gas stove burner.
Result: The fire heats the water. If left unattended, the heated water will evaporate into steam.

b. Air?
Scenario: A hurricane travels from Florida to New England.
Result: Air moves the water through the sky and disperses it over the East Coast.

c. Earth?
Scenario: Dirt is shoveled into a rain filled ditch.
Result: Earth blends with water and becomes mud.

3. How is Air Affected By:

a. Fire?
Scenario #1: A person lights a match in a gas filled room.
Result: An explosion.
Scenario #2: A person lights a match outdoors.
Result: The fire uses the oxygen in the air to create its flame.

b. Water?
Scenario: The air is saturated with water minutes before a thunderstorm.
Result: Loaded down with water, the air feels heavy.

c. Earth?
Scenario: An empty hole is filled in with gravel.
Result: Earth moves the air out of the hole and takes its place.

4. How is Earth Affected By:

a. Fire?
Scenario: A wooden house is on fire.
Result: The fire destroys the house.

b. Water?
Scenario: A sand dune is pounded repeatedly by ocean waves.
Result: The water gradually erodes away the sand dune.

c. Air?
Scenario: A tropical breeze makes the palm trees sway.
Result: Air can move earth.

PHYSICAL ELEMENTAL CONVERSATIONS

1. What Would Fire Say To:

a. Water? "Why do you always put me out?"
          "It's hard for me to burn when you rain on me."
          "I hate rainy days."

b. Air? "I need more air to grow larger."
          "Don't blow me out."

c. Earth? "Stop smothering me."
          "I need you for fuel."
          "You contain me."

2. What Would Water Say To:

a. Fire? "You heat me up!"
          "You agitate me!"
          "You make me boil!"
          "You steam me!"

b. Air? "You scatter me!"

c. Earth? "You give me form."
          "You contain me."

3. What Would Air Say To:

a. Fire? "You need me."
          "You use me."

b. Water? "You make me feel so heavy."

c. **Earth?** "Give me room to breathe!"
"You're pushing me out of my space!"

4. What Would Earth Say To:

a. **Fire?** "You use me, disfigure me, even destroy me."

b. **Water?** "You nourish me." (All plants need water.)
"You can gradually erode my form."
"In a flood, you can drastically alter my appearance."

c. **Air?** "You nourish me." (All plants need oxygen.)
"Your winds can move me."

THE ELEMENTS' PSYCHOLOGICAL EXPRESSIONS

If you need any help with this exercise, go back to the elemental keyword lists in Chapters 4-7.

PSYCHOLOGICAL INTERACTIONS

1. How Is Fire Affected By:

a. Water?
Keywords: Ambitious (fire)/Hidden (water)
Result: A secretly ambitious inidividual who keeps his dreams to himself.
Keywords: Adventurous (fire)/Fantasy(water)
Result: Exciting daydreams

b. Air?

Keywords: Arrogance (fire)/Mental (air)
Result: An intellectually arrogant person — a know it all.
Keywords: Energized (fire)/Sociable (air)
Result: An enthusiastic conversationalist.

c. Earth?

Keywords: Competitive (fire)/Stability (earth)
Result: A conservative individual who fights to maintain the status quo.
Keywords: Sexual (fire)/Inhibited (earth)
Result: A sexually repressed individual.

2. How Is Water Affected By:

a. Fire?

Keywords: Sensual (water)/Showy (fire)
Result: An individual who blatantly expresses his sensual nature.
Keywords: Psychic (water)/Independent (fire)
Result: A person who follows his psychic impressions, no matter what others think.

b. Air?

Keywords: Emotions (water)/Inquisitive (air)
Result: A person who is curious about human behavior.
Keywords: Dreamy (water)/Literary (air)
Result: An avid fan of romance novels.

c. Earth?

Keywords: Caring (water)/Reserved (earth)
Result: A person who doesn't easily share his emotions.
Keywords: Internal (water)/Controlled (earth)
Result: A person who tries to control his inner feelings.

3. How Is Air Affected By:

a. Fire?
Keywords: Talkative (air)/Action (fire)
Result: A person who wants to act on his ideas.
Keywords: Scientific (air)/Pioneer (fire)
Result: An inventor.

b. Water?
Keywords: Ideas (air)/Visionary (water)
Result: A futurist thinker.
Keywords: Storytelling (air)/Magickal (water)
Result: An individual who understands the power of myths.

c. Earth?
Keywords: Reasoning (air)/Economics (earth)
Result: A financial expert.
Keywords: Evaluate (air)/Commonsense (earth)
Result: An individual who approaches problems with a realistic attitude.

4. How Is Earth Affected By:

a. Fire?
Keywords: Materially-oriented (earth)/Ambitious (fire)
Result: A person who will strive for material success.
Keywords: Persistent (earth)/Willful (fire)
Result: This person never gives up! He wants his way!

b. Water?
Keywords: Responsibility (earth)/Soothing (water)
Result: A caretaker personality.
Keywords: Traditional (earth)/Emotional (water)
Result: A sentimental individual.

c. Air?
Keywords: Work (earth)/Analytical (air)
Result: A person who wants a job where he can use his mind.
Keywords: Ordered (earth)/Scientific (air)
Result: An individual who believes that life's events can be explained through scientific knowledge.

ELEMENTAL CONVERSATIONS: FROM A PSYCHOLOGICAL PERSPECTIVE

1. Fire To Water

Fire Keyword: Pushy
Water Keyword: Mellow
Fire's Comment: "How can you relax when there's so much to do!"
Water's Response: "I don't like rushing!"

2. Fire To Air

Fire Keyword: Decisive
Air Keyword: Indecisive
Fire's Comment: "I know what I want. Why can't you make up your mind?"
Air's Response: "Don't you understand that there are two sides to every story?"

3. Fire To Earth

Fire Keyword: Freedom-loving
Earth Keyword: Responsibility
Fire's Comment: "I hate the 9 to 5 routine. I wish I didn't have to work."

Earth's Response: "Let's be realistic. You have to work to pay your bills."

4. Water To Fire

Water Keyword: Feeling-oriented
Fire Keyword: Impatient
Water's Comment: "I'm not sure if I should do this. It doesn't feel right."
Fire's Response: "Make a decision — you don't have all day to figure out your feelings."

5. Water To Air

Water Keyword: Psychic
Air Keyword: Skeptic
Water's Comment: "There's a lot more to life than meets the eye!"
Air's Response: "I'll believe it when you can show me the evidence."

6. Water To Earth

Water Keyword: Caring
Earth Keyword: Work
Water's Comment: "You've been working a long time. Maybe you should take a short break."
Earth's Response: "Well, just a short break. I have a lot of work to do."

7. Air To Fire

Air Keyword: Thoughtful
Fire Keyword: Spontaneous

Air's Comment: "Don't you ever stop to think of the consequences of your actions?"

Fire's Response: "I don't like to think and plan ahead. I prefer to be spontaneous."

8. Air To Water

Air Keyword: Objective
Water Keyword: Emotions
Air's Comment: "You have to learn to be more objective and less sensitive."
Water's Response: "Stop rationalizing away emotions!"

9. Air To Earth

Air Keyword: Superficial conversationalist
Earth Keyword: Serious
Air's Comment: "You're too serious. Get out of your rut and go meet some new people."
Earth's Response: "I don't have time for silly chitchat."

10. Earth To Fire

Earth Keyword: Steady paced
Fire Keyword: High-Spirited
Earth's Comment: "Slow down and take it easy."
Fire's Response: "You're such a worrywart! I'm having fun!"

11. Earth To Water

Earth Keyword: Financially concerned
Water Keyword: Emotionally concerned

Earth's Comment: "So what if he doesn't fulfill you emotionally? He's rich!"

Water's Response: "Money's not everything. I need an inner connection."

12. Earth To Air

Earth Keyword: Grounded
Air Keyword: Contemplative
Earth's Comment: "Hello? Earth to space? Is anyone there?"
Air's Response: "What? Oh, I was just in deep thought."

Additional Comments On The Secondary Elements

Did you notice that there is a connection between a sign's secondary element and its quality? If not, take a minute to challenge yourself. Look at the chart below and see if you perceive the pattern.

Primary Elements	Secondary Elements			
	Fire	**Water**	**Air**	**Earth**
Fire		Leo	Sagittarius	Aries
Water	Scorpio		Pisces	Cancer
Air	Gemini	Aquarius		Libra
Earth	Capricorn	Taurus	Virgo	

Here's the pattern:

1. The signs with a secondary earth element are cardinal signs.
2. The signs with a secondary water element are fixed signs.
3. The signs with a secondary air element are mutable signs.
4. Only the secondary fire signs have one cardinal sign (Capricorn), one fixed sign (Scorpio), and one mutable sign (Gemini).

In conclusion, here are the:

Key Elements Of The Zodiac

	Glyph	Symbol	Primary Element	Secondary Element	Ruling Planet	Quality
Aries	♈	Ram	Fire	Earth	Mars	Cardinal
Taurus	♉	Bull	Earth	Water	Venus	Fixed
Gemini	♊	Twins	Air	Fire	Mercury	Mutable
Cancer	♋	Crab	Water	Earth	Moon	Cardinal
Leo	♌	Lion	Fire	Water	Sun	Fixed
Virgo	♍	Virgin	Earth	Air	Mercury	Mutable
Libra	♎	Scales	Air	Earth	Venus	Cardinal
Scorpio	♏	Scorpion Snake, Phoenix	Water	Fire	Pluto	Fixed
Sagittarius	♐	Centaur	Fire	Air	Jupiter	Mutable
Capricorn	♑	Mountain Goat & Sea Goat	Earth	Fire	Saturn	Cardinal
Aquarius	♒	Water Bearer	Air	Water	Uranus	Fixed
Pisces	♓	Two Fish	Water	Air	Neptune	Mutable

★ ▬▬▬▬ SERVICES AND PRODUCTS

Hello! I hope you enjoyed reading *Key Elements Of The Zodiac*. In the future I hope to share more astrological information through additional books and audio and video cassettes. If you're interested in my future products, please write to me and I'll be sure to put you on my mailing list.

There are two other things that I'd like to bring to your attention. First, as a professional astrologer, I provide astrological consulations. If you can't see me in person, I will tape your astrology reading on an audio cassette or give you a reading over the phone. If you're interested, details on my astrological consultations are given on the following pages.

Second, I also distribute Richard A. Greene's book, *The Handbook of Astral Power*, and his many tapes on subjects ranging from psychic healing to past lives to personal power (to mention just a few). A complete listing of his products is contained in this section as well.

If you have any questions at all regarding my astrological consultations or Richard Greene's book and tapes, please feel free to call me at (603) 880-6078 or write me at:

Stellar Communications
P.O. Box 1403
Nashua, NH 03061

Astrological Consultations

—————————WHAT DO MY READINGS COVER?

All my astrological readings take a look at your present situation and a look at the upcoming life cycles for the year ahead. Many times people are confused about the direction of their life because they are missing important pieces of information and consequently, can't see things clearly. With an astrological consultation you have the opportunity to understand your present life cycles from an objective, wholistic framework. Not only can I help you put things in perspective, I will also give you specific dates on when particular issues will peak in the year ahead.

Think of it this way. **Your astrological chart is like a roadmap, but you – not the planets – are in the driver's seat.** With the insights from your *personal* roadmap, you can make better decisions regarding your life issues.

—————————THE INFORMATION I NEED
TO DO YOUR CHART

In order to do an astrological consultation for you, I need to know three things:

1. **Your birthdate**
2. **Your birthplace**
3. **Your birth time**

If you don't know what time you were born, check your birth certificate or call the hospital you were born in. Some hospitals will give the information over the phone for free. Other hospitals require that you send a small fee first before they look up your birth records.

If you were not born in a hospital and your birth time is not on your birth certificate, perhaps it's listed in a baby book or a family Bible. Or maybe one of your relatives remembers the time. However, don't worry if there's no way you can locate your birth time. I can still do a reading for you and tell you some very specific things about yourself and your present life cycles.

————————HOW TO MAKE AN APPOINTMENT

A reading can be done in person or by mail. I encourage you to see me in person if you can because then you can participate in the reading.

If it's not possible to see me in person, then I can put your reading on an audio tape cassette and mail it to you. When you order a reading by mail, be sure to include any specific questions you have and any pertinent background information (i.e. Are you single or married?). Also, please note that I charge $10 extra for readings by mail. (This includes the cost of tapes, postage and handling.)

For an in-person reading, give me a call at (603) 880-6078 to set up an appointment. For a reading by mail or by phone, please send a check (no cash, please!) along with your birth information and personal background to: Stellar Communications, P.O. Box 1403, Nashua, N.H. 03061.

————————THE PRICES FOR MY READINGS
ARE AS FOLLOWS:*

1.) 60 MINUTES   — $75 ($85 BY MAIL)
2.) 90 MINUTES   — $100 ($110 BY MAIL)
3.) 120 MINUTES   — $125 ($135 BY MAIL)

* NOTE: These prices are subject to change without notice.

If you have any questions at all, please call me at (603) 880-6078.

**STELLAR COMMUNICATIONS PRODUCT
AND PRICE LIST
P.O. BOX 1403
NASHUA, NEW HAMPSHIRE 03061
(603) 880-6078**

$9.95 Key Elements Of The Zodiac, by Virginia Kay Miller
    Designed for individuals who seek to experience Astrology from an intuitive, feeling, right brain perspective. With original information and unique learning strategies it will challenge you to use your personal power to transform your astrological knowledge.

———— AUDIO TAPES BY RICHARD A. GREENE

These are the original lectures as given by Richard A. Greene who has pioneered research into the Mind and Spirit of Man. Each tape presents a new level of information and data about the spiritual abilities which lie dormant in most people. Now you can awaken your inner spirit and find the truth about yourself, life, this universe, planet Earth, your purpose here and much more. These tapes are your starting point on your next step in the journey of life.

ASTRAL PROJECTION

$9.95 1. The Real You – Beyond the Body
    This lecture reveals the immortal YOU. When the body dies, you will still exist...but who are you then? This tape answers this and other questions.

$9.95 2. How To Astral Project Through Distance and Space
    This lecture reveals the techniques to project your consciousness over distance no matter whether it be next door or millions of miles through space.

$9.95 3. How To Astral Project Through Time
Time travel through astral projection. This tape teaches you how!

$9.95 4. How To Astral Project Into Past Lives
Use astral projection techniques to remember your past lives! A remarkable tape!

PSYCHIC HEALING AND PSYCHIC ENERGY

$9.95 5. The Life Force Energy – How To Develop And Direct It
The Life Force Energy surrounds and animates all living things. This tape teaches you how to use the LFE in your everyday life to increase your physical vitality, reduce stress and much, much more.

$9.95 6. Psychic Healing – Healing Through Color,
Auras and The Life Force Energy
This tape teaches you how to use the Life Force Energy along with colors and the aura, in order to positively influence your own health and the health of others.

HIDDEN KNOWLEDGE

$9.95 7. The True Purpose of Planet Earth
Some people think earth is a classroom, but this tape may just change your mind. In this tape, you learn techniques to go back in time to when you, as an immortal soul, first came to planet Earth, and for what purpose.

$9.95 8. The Mysteries Of This Universe
In order to be a spiritually evolved person, and use your spiritual abilities, you must know something about the universe you are presently existing in. In this tape, you will learn the factors that create this universe as well as other ones.

$9.95 9. How To Obtain Personal Power

Many people feel that they do not have the power to control or change their lives. This tape teaches you the laws of personal power so you can have power in your life now. Empower yourself!

$9.95 10. What Really Happens Between Lifetimes

It is interesting how many books have been written about past lives but nobody seems to know the truth about what happens in the "between lifetimes period." This is very vital and important information for your spiritual development.

$9.95 11. The True Story Behind Karma and Reincarnation

By understanding how karma and reincarnation actually work, you will have a greater awareness of your present strengths, weaknesses, and goals.

PSYCHIC AND SPIRITUAL DEVELOPMENT

$9.95 12. How To Develop and Use Telepathy

Telepathy is the communication process of sending thoughts, images, and energy from one person's mind to another mind. This tape teaches you the techniques to develop telepathy. So who needs telephones?

$9.95 13. How To Develop and Use Psychokinesis

Psychokinesis is the ability to use your mind to influence and affect matter such as bending metal keys, or moving objects using only thought. This tape teaches you the techniques to develop the power of psychokinesis.

$9.95 14. How To See Auras

Auras are the energy fields that surround all living things. By learning to see auras, you can tell the emotional, mental and physical status of any individual. All the techniques you need to see auras are included in this tape.

$9.95 15. How To Communicate With Your Higher Self

The Higher Self is your true inner spiritual being. When you are in touch with your Higher Self, you are in touch with the highest levels of spiritual knowledge and being. This tape teaches you how to communicate with your spiritual Higher Self.

PSYCHIC POWERS

$9.95 16. How To Develop Invisibility

Invisibility is the ability to alter your features by using the Life Force Energy to change the way that light emits from your aura. This tape teaches you how it is done!

$9.95 17. How to Develop and Use Your Psychic Powers

This tape explains what psychic powers are, how and why they work, and how to develop them. Some of the abilities covered are telepathy and psychic healing.

$9.95 18. How To Attract Wealth and Prosperity

Few people understand the laws of wealth and prosperity. This is one of the reasons why most people lack the wealth they desire. This tape contains exercises to prepare your consciousness to attract the very wealth and the $$$ you need!

$9.95 19. How To Handle The Problems In Your Life

Wouldn't it be nice to finally handle the problems in your life so that you can stop worrying and move on to more productive and fun things? This tape teaches you what a problem really is, and the methods to solve each and every problem that is in your life. This tape is a must!

$9.95 20. Death – The Final Mystery

What is death? Why does it happen? What occurs after death? This tape contains exercises and data researched through past life therapy by Richard Greene. Included in this tape are exercises to help you overcome the grief, fear and worry associated with death.

$9.95 21. How To Control Time
What is time? Where does it come from? These questions and more are asked and answered in this tape. As you learn and understand the source of where time comes from, you are also taught how to control time to get things done.

$9.95 22. How To Gain Control Of Your Life
At some point in our lives, we all go through a time where we feel that we have lost the purpose which is the very reason why we are on this planet. This is when we feel out of control. This tape explains how and why we lose control of our life and the techniques necessary to regain control. This is an important tape!

$9.95 23. How To Manifest The Things You Want In Your Life
It seems that very few people ever get what they want out of life. People who do are using laws of consciousness whether they realize it or not. This tape teaches you all the laws necessary to bring your wishes and dreams into reality. A "must have" tape!!!

—————————————BOOK BY RICHARD A. GREENE

$14.95 The Handbook of Astral Power
Formerly titled *The Handbook of Astral Projection*, this book is the classic on astral projection developed by Richard A. Greene. It actually teaches you how to astral project using easy to learn techniques that have been developed over two decades. Also covered are important uses of astral projection for pain control, stress reduction and much more. In addition, you can see your progress in astral projection by taking the TOUR GUIDE TO THE SUN AND MOON test at the end of the book.

STELLAR COMMUNICATIONS PRODUCT ORDER FORM
P.O. BOX 1403
NASHUA, NEW HAMPSHIRE 03061
(603) 880-6078

Please mail this order form with the products you desire checked off. Make all money payable in U.S. dollars, please. VISA and MasterCard orders are also welcome.

Include $2.00 for Postage and Handling!

ASTROLOGY

___$9.95 *Key Elements Of The Zodiac*

ASTRAL PROJECTION

___$9.95 1. The Real You – Beyond The Body

___$9.95 2. How To Astral Project Through
               Distance and Space

___$9.95 3. How To Astral Project Through Time

___$9.95 4. How To Astral Project Into Past Lives

___$9.95 5. The Life Force Energy – How to
              Develop And Direct It

___$9.95 6. Psychic Healing – Healing Through
              Colors, Auras, and the Life Force Energy

HIDDEN KNOWLEDGE

___$9.95 7. The True Purpose of Planet Earth

___$9.95 8. The Mysteries Of This Universe

___$9.95 9. How To Obtain Personal Power

___$9.95 10. What Really Happens Between Lifetimes

___$9.95 11. The True Story Behind Karma
          and Reincarnation

PSYCHIC AND SPIRITUAL DEVELOPMENT

___$9.95 12. How To Develop and Use Telepathy

___$9.95 13. How To Develop and Use Psychokinesis

___$9.95 14. How To See Auras

___$9.95 15. How To Communicate With Your Higher Self

PSYCHIC POWERS

___$9.95 16. How To Develop Invisibility

___$9.95 17. How To Develop And Use Your Psychic Powers

___$9.95 18. How To Attract Wealth and Prosperity

___$9.95 19. How To Handle The Problems In Your Life

___$9.95 20. Death – The Final Mystery

___$9.95 21. How To Control Time

___$9.95 22. How To Gain Control Of Your Life

___$9.95 23. How To Manifest The Things You
          Want In Your LIfe

BOOK BY RICHARD A. GREENE

___ **$14.95 The Handbook of Astral Power**

AUDIO CASSETTE TAPE COURSES

___ **$39.95 The Astral Projection Course - Level 1**
     This course includes audio tapes #2, #3, #4, and *The Handbook of Astral Power*. Save over $5.00

___ **$69.95 The Communication Course - Level 1**
           (Consists of 6 one hour tapes)
     Includes information and techniques on the cycles of communication, how to influence others via communication, communicate with others telepathically, and so much more.

Video & Audio Cassette Tape Courses

Many new video and audio cassette courses are being developed. Call (603) 880-6078 for titles and prices.

Name:_____
                          (Please Print)

Address:_____

City & State:_____

Zip:_____

Tel. #: (   )_____

MasterCard/Visa #: _____

Expiration Date:_____